Mastering

Real Estate

Investment

Examples, Metrics and Case Studies

Frank Gallinelli

RealData, Inc.
Southport, CT

608-100

ISBN 0-9818138-0-1

CONTENTS

Introduction 1

Part One: 37 Key Real Estate Measures – Examples and Metrics

Chapter 1: Simple Interest 1

Chapter 2: Compound Interest...4

Chapter 3: Rule of 72s 7

Chapter 4: Present Value of a Future Cash Flow...................................9

Chapter 5: Gross Rent Multiplier 13

Chapter 6: Gross Scheduled Income (Potential Gross Income) 17

Chapter 7: Vacancy and Credit Loss Allowance 22

Chapter 8: Gross Operating Income (Effective Gross Income).............. 27

Chapter 9: Net Operating Income 30

Chapter 10: Capitalization Rate.. 37

Chapter 11: Net Income Multiplier 42

Chapter 12: Taxable Income 44

Chapter 13: Cash Flow 51

Chapter 14: Cash-on-Cash Return... 59

Chapter 15: Sale Proceeds... 64

Chapter 16: Discounted Cash Flow 70

Chapter 17: Net Present Value.. 75

Chapter 18: Profitability Index... 80

Chapter 19: Internal Rate of Return... 84

Chapter 20: Price, Income, and Expenses per Unit 87

Chapter 21: Price, Income, and Expenses per Square Foot 89

Chapter 22: Operating Expense Ratio 92

Chapter 23: Debt Coverage Ratio 97

Chapter 24: Break-Even Ratio 101

Chapter 25: Return on Equity 106

Chapter 26: Loan-to-Value Ratio 109

Chapter 27: Points 113

Chapter 28: Mortgage Payment / Mortgage Constant 115

Chapter 29: Principal Balance / Balloon Payment 120

Chapter 30: Principal and Interest per Period 126

Chapter 31: Maximum Loan Amount 130

Chapter 32: Assessed Value, Property Taxes, and Value Indicated by

Assessment 134

Chapter 33: Adjusted Basis 136

Chapter 34: Depreciation 139

Chapter 35: Gain on Sale 143

Chapter 36: Land Measurements 146

Chapter 37: Building Measurements 149

Part Two: Case Studies

Chapter 38: The Single-Family House 155

Chapter 39: The Single Family, Redeveloped 171

Chapter 40: The Apartment Complex 187

Chapter 41: The Shopping Center 205

Index 247

Introduction

When I finished writing *What Every Real Estate Investor Needs to Know About Cash Flow* (McGraw-Hill, 2004), my first official act was to lower my expectations for its success. Really, who is going to curl up by the fire with a book that is filled with numbers and formulas?

To my surprise, and even greater delight, a lot of people seem to have done exactly that. As I write this, it has been almost five years since the release of the book, and it's still going strong. My goal was to stay completely away from the motivational, quick-rich-quick hype that causes bookstore shelves to sag, and instead focus on teaching how income-property investments really work. How do you run the numbers to decide if the property in front of you might turn out to be a successful investment or a dud?

Since the publication of that book I've been fortunate to receive quite a number of emails with questions, comments and suggestions, and it is from my dialog with readers that this new book has emerged. In short, you asked for a lot more examples, practice exercises and case studies with which you could sharpen your analytical skills. So here they are.

I've divided this book into two sections. In the first, I revisit the 37 key measures I described in the *Cash Flow* book. My approach in this section may provoke flashbacks to your childhood piano teacher, but my purpose is to provide you with mastery exercises. These chapters are filled with sample problems and solutions illustrating each of those 37 measures and giving you opportunities to practice them. If, as my title suggests, you are going to master real estate investment, you must first master these key measures.

In the second section of the book I focus more on how actually to analyze real estate investments. I start with what may be the smallest – though potentially problematic – of property investments, the single-family home. From there I work my way up the food chain, to a renovation project, an apartment building, and finally a small shopping center.

My goal in these case studies is to show you how to build and interpret proforma projections of each property's potential future performance. To do so, I frequently display the output of software produced by my company, RealData (http://www.realdata.com). From time to time, I edit the output of those programs so what you see on the page focuses strictly on the issues in the case study.

You don't necessarily have to use my company's software to analyze the sample properties. Be aware, however, that if you use some other software this book may spontaneously combust. If you have an ample supply of pencils and calculator batteries, you could even run the numbers manually.

I also provide a website – http://www.realdata.com/book – where you may download free tools that can help you when you need to do something like a mortgage calculation or a simple Discounted Cash Flow.

It's not really my purpose in this second section, however, to teach you how to use any particular software package or even how to figure the projections by hand. What's more important is that you start to develop a feel for how you should approach these analyses, how to look for the important clues, and how to make some sense of the numbers.

Real estate is a competitive business. Success in real estate – or in anything worthwhile – is not automatic or guaranteed. I believe, however, that if you take the material in this book to heart, you'll develop a sound and analytical approach to your investing. It's an approach that requires some effort, discipline and commitment, but one that will help you make the best and most informed investment choices.

Frank Gallinelli

Part One

37 Key Real Estate Measures

Examples and Metrics

1

Simple Interest

S imple interest is exactly that: simple. You apply the rate of interest always to the original principal amount only. Contrast this to the concept in the next chapter, compound interest.

You can calculate the interest with the first formula below; or, by using the second formula, you can figure the total to which a starting amount of principal grows.

Interest = Principal x Rate x Time

Amount = Principal x [1 + (Rate x Time)]

Problem 1-1:

You invest $5,000 at 5% annual simple interest for 5 years. At the end of the term, how much interest have you earned in dollars?

Problem 1-2:

You loan $3,750 to your best friend. Soon you will be looking for a new best friend. In the meantime, he will be obliged to give you simple interest only, at 12% per annum, payable on a monthly basis. How much do you expect him to pay each year?

Problem 1-3:

You borrow $6,250 from your mother-in-law. She never liked you all that much anyway, so the interest rate is 16% per annum, payable quarterly. Your payments are simple interest only and your first payment is due September 1. How much interest will you have paid (on a cash basis) by the end of the first calendar year (i.e., by December 31)?

Problem 1-4:

You deposit $10,000 in a bank that pays 5% simple interest per year. How much will you have in your account at the end of 3½ years?

Answer 1-1:

Apply the formula, Interest = Principal x Rate x Time

$5,000 \times 0.05 \times 5 = 1,250$

Answer 1-2:

$3,750 \times 0.01 \times 12 = 450$

Since there are no principal payments to reduce the balance against which interest will be calculated, you will pay the same amount whether you make 12 payments at the monthly rate of 1% each or one payment at the annual rate of 12% as shown below

$3,750 \times 0.12 \times 1 = 450$

Answer 1-3:

First you must calculate the quarterly rate of interest. Since the annual rate is 16%, the quarterly rate is 4%.

Next you need to determine how many payments you will make between the time the loan commences and December 31. The first payment is September 1 and the next quarterly payment will be December 1. Hence, you will make two payments before the end of the year. Interest is accruing during December, of course, but you will not actually pay that until your next quarterly payment comes due in February.

Finally you need to calculate the amount of each interest payment and multiply it by the number of payments to be made:

6,250 x 0.04 x 2 = 500

Answer 1-4:

You need to apply the second formula shown above.

Final Amount = Principal x [1 + (Rate x Time)]

10,000 x [1 + (0.05 x 3.5)]

10,000 x [1 + 0.175]

10.000 x 1.175 = 11,750

2

Compound Interest

C ompound interest differs from simple interest in one key respect: With compound interest you apply the interest rate not only to the original principal but also to the accumulated interest.

You can use the first formula below to calculate the Future Value, i.e., the original principal plus accumulated interest. You can also calculate the Future Value longhand, by stepping through one period at a time. Use the second formula to figure the total interest that accrues over time.

Future Value = Principal x (1 + Periodic Rate) ^ Number of Periods

Total Interest = Future Value - Original Principal

Problem 2-1:

You take $1,000 to the bank and deposit it in an account that pays 6% interest compounded annually. Use the longhand method to calculate what your account balance should be at the end of two years.

Problem 2-2:

You find a better bank. They also pay 6% per year, but compound it quarterly. You pull your money out of the first bank at the end of the first year there, give them back their free toaster, and put the full proceeds into the second bank. Use the first formula above to calculate how much will you have after your money has been in the old bank for one year and the new bank for two years.

Problem 2-3:

How much interest did you earn after one year in the first bank? How much after two years in the second bank?

Problem 2-4:

If you had put $1,000 in each bank for one year, how much more interest would you have earned in the second bank because of its more frequent compounding?

Answer 2-1:

You start with $1,000 and earn 6% ($60.00) in the first year. At the beginning of the second year you have $1,060 in your account, which earns 6% ($63.60), so your account balance at the end of that year should be $1,123.60.

Year	Starting Balance	Interest	Ending Balance
1	1,000.00	60.00	1,060.00
2	1,060.00	63.60	1,123.60

Answer 2-2:

You'll be taking your money out of the bank above at the end of the first year, so your starting principal with the new bank is $1,060. A 6% annual interest rate compounded quarterly means 1.5% applied each quarter, so 1.5% is the periodic rate for each of eight periods.

Apply the formula, Principal x (1 + Periodic Rate) ^ Number of Periods

Future Value = 1,060.00 x (1 + 0.015) ^ 8

Future Value = 1,060.00 x (1.015 x 1.015 x 1.015 x 1.015 x 1.015 x 1.015 x 1.015 x 1.015)

Future Value = 1,060.00 x 1.126493

Future Value = 1,194.08

Answer 2-3:

To determine the interest earned, subtract what you started with from what you ended up with. Apply the formula, Total Interest = Future Value - Original Principal.

Total interest, by End of Year 1, Bank #1 = 1,060.00 – 1,000 = 60.00

Total interest, after Years 2 and 3, Bank #2 = 1,194.08 – 1,000 = 194.08

Answer 2-4:

You already know that $1,000 invested in Bank #1 would earn $60 in one year.

For Bank #2, apply the formula, Principal x (1 + Periodic Rate) ^ Number of Periods

Future Value = 1,000.00 x (1 + 0.015) ^ 4

Future Value = 1,000.00 x 1.015 x 1.015 x 1.015 x 1.015

Future Value = 1,000.00 x 1.061364

Future Value = 1,061.36

Then apply the formula, Total Interest = Future Value - Original Principal

Total Interest = 1,061.36 – 1,000.00 = 61.36

You would have earned $60.00 with Bank #1's annual compounding, but $61.36 with Bank #2's quarterly compounding, a difference of $1.36.

3

Rule of 72s

T he rule of 72s will give you the approximate number of years required to double your investment at a given rate of growth. This bit of mental gymnastics is useful when you haven't got a calculator – or even a pencil – handy, so try these problems in your head.

Number of Years to Double in Value (approx.) = 72 / Rate of Growth

Problem 3-1:

You have just purchased a new home, and the oracle at Delphi assures you that home values will rise at 10% per year for the foreseeable future. About how many years will it take for your home to double in value? Are you sure that wasn't a kid in a Halloween costume?

Problem 3-2:

You open a bank account into which you plan to deposit all of your future lottery winnings. The account pays 6% compounded annually. How long will it take for your first deposit to double in value?

Answer 3-1:

Apply the formula:

Number of Years to Double in Value (approx.) = 72 / Rate of Growth.

You can divide any number by 10 without resorting to long division. At a 10% growth rate, your home would double in value in about 7.2 years.

Answer 3-2:

If you wait to win the lottery, you may be waiting forever to make that first deposit; but if you do put money in at 6%, then

Number of Years to Double in Value (approx.) = 72 / 6

Number of Years to Double in Value (approx.) = 12 years

4

Present Value of a Future Cash Flow

Y ou can think of calculating Present Value (PV) as the reverse of the compound interest process. With compound interest you know the Present Value (i.e., the starting amount) and you know the periodic interest rate; you are trying to find what you would end up with – the Future Value (FV).

With this new calculation you still know the periodic rate but now you know the FV and want to figure out the PV instead.

As an investor, you have a very specific reason for wanting to make this calculation. Most investment returns, especially with real estate, do not arrive instantly. You may have to wait several years until you sell a property and realize a return. The longer you have to wait for a return, the less valuable it is because during that period of waiting you did not have the return in hand to put to work elsewhere. Money received in the future is less valuable than money received today. Hence, you use discounting to find the present worth (the PV) of a future return (the FV).

Present Value = Future Value / $[(1 + i)^n]$, where i is the periodic discount rate and n is the number of periods

The formula can be cumbersome to use, but there are other ways you can make this calculation. One method is to use a table of Annual Present Value Factors, which we provide at http://www.realdata.com/book. If you use the table, your formula works as follows:

Present Value = Factor from Table x Future Value

Another way to get your answer is to use Microsoft Excel's built-in function, PV. The function looks like this:

=PV(rate,nper,pmt,fv,type).

Rate is the interest rate per period; **nper** is the number of periods; **pmt** is the amount of periodic payments, which we will not use here; **fv** is the Future Value; and **type** designates whether payments are made at the beginning or the end of periods. You don't need to use this last item, because the default is what you want here: end-of-period.

You will see both the PV table and the Excel methods demonstrated below.

Problem 4-1:

I promise that I will give you $1,000 three years from today. You appreciate my generosity, but at the same time you recognize that if I gave you the money to-day you could invest it at 5%. What is the value today of this promised $1,000?

Problem 4-2:

You are considering the purchase of a property that will generate no yearly cash flows but will yield $100,000 cash proceeds upon sale five years from today. You believe that alternative investment opportunities would give you 10% per year return on your money. What is the greatest amount of cash you would be willing to commit to this investment?

Answer 4-1:

Solve this problem first by using the table of Present Value Factors located at http://www.realdata.com/book. You'll find the table among the pdf files there.

5

Gross Rent Multiplier

G ross Rent Multiplier (GRM) is a market-driven measurement that expresses the ratio of Market Value to Gross Scheduled Income. If you know the multiplier that prevails in a particular market, you can apply it to the Gross Scheduled Income of a subject property to estimate the Market Value of that property.

The most common use of GRM is to estimate the value of small (2-4 unit) multi-family properties.

Gross Rent Multiplier = Market Value / Gross Scheduled Income (annual)

Market Value = Gross Rent Multiplier x Gross Scheduled Income (annual)

Problem 5-1:

You own a three-family house with a Gross Scheduled Income of $22,500. A local appraiser advises you that the typical Gross Rent Multiplier in your neighborhood is 7.1. If the appraiser uses the GRM to estimate value, then what value might she estimate for this property? What other appraisal techniques might she consider using, and why might they be appropriate (or inappropriate)?

Problem 5-2:

During the past six months you observed the following transactions among multi-family properties in a particular neighborhood:

Gross Scheduled Income	Selling Price
28,400	207,500
32,000	240,000
25,940	185,000
27,150	195,000
30,225	220,000

What was the Gross Rent Multiplier exhibited by each of these sales? What was average GRM for the neighborhood?

Problem 5-3:

You are considering the purchase of a property similar to those above, in the same neighborhood. You have three candidates in mind, each with a different Gross Scheduled Income:

Gross Scheduled Income

27,900
29,500
31,750

Using the average Gross Rent Multiplier from the previous problem, what is your estimate of the Market Value for each of these properties? Also use the high and low GRMs from that problem to estimate a range of potential values. Round to the nearest thousand.

Answer 5-1:

Apply the formula, Market Value = Gross Rent Multiplier x Gross Scheduled
Income:

Market Value = 22,500 x 7.1

Market Value = 159,750

Appraisers will generally use a Market Data Approach, Income Approach, or
Cost Approach to value.

If the multi-family properties in this neighborhood are mostly owner-occupied,
then their values may behave more like single-family homes than investment
properties. In that case, the appraiser may look at comparable sales and adjust
for differences in amenities (such as number of bedrooms, number of bath-
rooms, etc.), overall size and condition.

If the properties in the neighborhood are predominantly investments, perhaps
mixed with some commercial, such as office and retail, then the appraiser might
prefer an income capitalization approach instead of GRM (see Chapter 10 for a
discussion of capitalization rates).

The cost approach (cost to rebuild, less accumulated physical depreciation) is
also an option, but is probably less likely because multi-family homes tend to be
older and the cost approach is more reliable with newer properties.

Answer 5-2:

Apply the formula, Gross Rent Multiplier = Market Value / Gross Scheduled
Income to fill in the blanks:

Gross Scheduled Income	Selling Price	GRM
28,400	207,500	7.31
32,000	240,000	7.50
25,940	185,000	7.13
27,150	195,000	7.18
30,225	220,000	7.28

Average = (7.31 + 7.50 + 7.13 + 7.18 + 7.28) / 5

Average = 7.28

Answer 5-3:

Apply the formula, Market Value = Gross Rent Multiplier x Gross Scheduled Income. Use the average GRM to declare a single answer, but also use the high and low GRMs to give yourself a sense of the possible range of values. Remember that you are rounding to the nearest thousand.

Gross Scheduled Income	Value with Average GRM	Value with Range of GRMs
27,900	203,000	199,000 – 209,000
29,500	215,000	210,000 – 221,000
31,750	231,000	226,000 – 238,000

6

Gross Scheduled Income (Potential Gross Income)

T his and the next several chapters should not tax your computational skills very much, but that doesn't mean the topics are trivial. The purpose of this book is to review and practice each of the concepts in my *Cash Flow* book, not to contrive a high-impact math workout. With some of these concepts, a computer is helpful; with others, a stubby pencil should do.

Gross Scheduled Income (aka Potential Gross Income) is a property's gross income assuming all space is actually rented. To express it as a formula:

Gross Scheduled Income = Total annual rent payable for occupied space plus total potential rent, at market rates, for vacant space

Problem 6-1:

You own a fully occupied three-family house with rents of $600, $700 and $800 per month. What is your property's Gross Scheduled Income?

Problem 6-2:

Today is January 1. You own that same three-family in Problem. 6-1, but the rent for each apartment will increase by $50 on July 1. What is your property's Gross Scheduled Income for the current calendar year?

Problem 6-3:

You were so successful running that three-family that you decided to buy a 40-unit apartment complex. You have eight studio apartments, 22 one-bedroom units, and 10 two-bedroom units. One of the studios is vacant, as are two of the one-bedroom units. The studios are rented for $800 each, the one-bedrooms for $900 and the two-bedrooms for $1,000 per month. The market rent of the vacant units is $50 more than the rent of the similar occupied units. What is your property's Gross Scheduled Income?

Problem 6-4:

There's no stopping you. You sell the three-family and the apartment building and reinvest in a mixed-use project downtown. The rent roll looks like this:

Unit type	Occupied	@Rent	Vacant	@Market Rent
Studio Apartments	10	950/mo	2	1,050/mo
1- bedroom	12	1,250/mo	2	1,350/mo
2-bedroom	6	1,700/mo	1	1,800/mo
Retail	3,000 sf	50.00/sf		
Retail	4,500 sf	47.50/sf		
Retail			4,000 sf	50.00/sf
Office	1,000 sf	32.00/sf		
Office			1,200 sf	32.00/sf

What is your property's Gross Scheduled Income?

Answer 6-1:

There is no vacant space, so the Gross Scheduled Income is simply the annual rental income, $25,200:

600 x 12 = 7,200   ($600 per month times 12 months)
700 x 12 = 8,400
800 x 12 = 9,600
              25,200

Answer 6-2:

Again there are no vacant units to account for, but you must pro-rate the rent for each unit, six months at the original rent and six months at the increased amount.

600 x 6 = 3,600   ($600 per month times 6 months)
650 x 6 = 3,900

700 x 6 = 4,200
750 x 6 = 4,500

800 x 6 = 4,800
<u>850 x 6 = 5,100</u>
         26,100

Answer 6-3:

Your apartment building has seven studios occupied at $800 per month, one vacant at a fair market value of $850; 20 one-bedrooms occupied at $900, two vacant at $950; and 10 two-bedrooms, all occupied at $1,000.

800 x 12 x 7 =   67,200   ($800 per month x 12 months x 7 units)

850 x 12 x 1 =   10,200

900 x 12 x 20 =   216,000

950 x 12 x 2 =   22,800

<u>1,000 x 12 x 10 = 120,000</u>
              436,200

Your annual Gross Scheduled Income is $436,200

Answer 6-4:

In this problem, you have residential units, whose rent is expressed in dollars per month, and commercial (i.e., non-residential) space, whose rent is expressed in dollars per square foot per year.

Let's start with the residential space:

Unit type	Occupied	@Rent	Vacant	@Market Rent
Studio Apartments	10	950/mo	2	1,050/mo
1- bedroom	12	1,250/mo	2	1,350/mo
2-bedroom	6	1,700/mo	1	1,800/mo

You total these rents as follows:

$$950 \times 12 \times 10 \ = \ 114,000$$
$$1,050 \times 12 \times 2 \ = \ 25,200$$

$$1,250 \times 12 \times 12 \ = \ 180,000$$
$$1,350 \times 12 \times 2 \ = \ 32,400$$

$$1,700 \times 12 \times 6 \ = \ 122,400$$
$$\underline{1,800 \times 12 \times 1 \ = \ \ \ 21,600}$$
$$495,600$$

The residential portion of your mixed-use property has a Gross Schedule Income of $495,600. Now for the commercial part:

Unit type	Occupied	@Rent	Vacant	@Market Rent
Retail	3,000 sf	50.00/sf		
Retail	4,500 sf	47.50/sf		
Retail			4,000 sf	50.00/sf
Office	1,000 sf	32.00/sf		
Office			1,200 sf	32.00/sf

You calculate the annual rent by multiplying the area times the rate per square foot.

3,000 x 50.00 = 150,000 (3,000 square feet times $50 per square foot per year)

4,500 x 47.50 = 213,750
4,000 x 50.00 = 200,000
1,000 x 32.00 = 32,000
1,200 x 32.00 = 38,400
              634,150

Note that you have taken into account both the occupied space at its actual rent and the vacant space at its fair market rent.

Your combined Gross Scheduled Income for the residential units and the commercial space is $495,600 plus $634,150, or $1,129,750. You've certainly come a long way since you ran that three-family house.

7

Vacancy and Credit Loss Allowance

A s the problems in the previous section make abundantly clear, not every residential unit or every square foot of commercial space stays occupied one hundred percent of the time. Or, if it does, then people are giggling behind your back because your rents are so low you couldn't get your tenants to budge with a stink bomb.

It is fair to presume that your perfect-world Gross Scheduled Income will be depleted by vacancy loss. It may also be reduced by something called credit loss, which is a polite term for those individuals or businesses who do indeed occupy your property but somehow fail to pay you for that privilege.

In the current or a past year you might report your loss as the actual dollar amount you experienced. If you are making projections regarding your property's performance in the future, then in most cases you will estimate your loss as a percentage of the property's Gross Scheduled Income. When you do so, you typically call it something like Vacancy and Credit Loss Allowance to indicate that it is indeed an allowance, a cushion to deal with the probability of lost income. In that case, the formula is simply

Vacancy and Credit Loss Allowance = Gross Scheduled Income x estimated % vacancy and credit loss

Problem 7-1:

What is the actual dollar amount of vacancy loss in Problems 6-3 and 6-4, above? What is your vacancy loss percentage in each? For Problem 6-4, break down the vacancy according to residential and commercial space, as well as for the property overall.

Problem 7-2:

You own a fully-occupied building with 10 units, each renting for $800 per month. You estimate that in the next 12 months you might have a 3% vacancy and credit loss. If you are correct, then what will the dollar amount of your loss be?

Problem 7-3:

You own a building with eight units whose actual and fair market rental is $900 per month. Last year, one of the units was vacant for two months. What was your vacancy loss percentage?

Problem 7-4:

You own a fully occupied building with six units, each renting for $750 per month. Last year, one of your tenants skipped out of the last month of his lease, leaving a bad check on the refrigerator door. What was your percentage of vacancy and credit loss?

Answer 7-1:

Recall the breakdown of rental units from problem 6-3:

    800 x 12 x 7 = 67,200
    850 x 12 x 1 = 10,200 vacant

    900 x 12 x 20 = 216,000

950 x 12 x 2 = 22,800 vacant

$\underline{1,000 \times 12 \times 10 = 120,000}$
                          436,200

The three vacant units represent $33,000 in rent. 33,000 divided by the Gross Scheduled Income of 436,200 yields a vacancy loss of 7.6%.

Problem 6-4 had both residential and commercial space:

Unit type	Occupied	@Rent	Vacant	@Market Rent
Studio Apartments	10	950/mo	2	1,050/mo
1- bedroom	12	1,250/mo	2	1,350/mo
2-bedroom	6	1,700/mo	1	1,800/mo

Unit type	Occupied	@Rent	Vacant	@Market Rent
Retail	3,000 sf	50.00/sf		
Retail	4,500 sf	47.50/sf		
Retail			4,000 sf	50.00/sf
Office	1,000 sf	32.00/sf		
Office			1,200 sf	32.00/sf

The vacant residential space:

1,050 x 12 x 2 = 25,200
1,350 x 12 x 2 = 32,400
$\underline{1,800 \times 12 \times 1 = 21,600}$
                        79,200

The residential space had a total Gross Scheduled Income of $495,600. The percentage of vacancy loss for just the residential space, therefore, is 79,200 divided by 495,600, or 16%.

The vacant commercial space:
   4,000 x 50.00 = 200,000
   $\underline{1,200 \times 32.00 = \quad 38,400}$
                           238,400

The commercial space had a total Gross Scheduled Income of $634,150. The percentage of vacancy loss for just the commercial space, therefore, is 238,400 divided by 634,150, or 37.6%.

Overall, the property had vacancy loss of $317,600 (79,200 plus 238,400) against a total Gross Scheduled Income of $1,129,750 (495,600 plus 634,150). The percentage of vacancy loss for the entire property, therefore, is 317,600 divided by 1,129,750, or 28.1%.

Answer 7-2:

The total Gross Scheduled Income for the property is

800 x 12 x 10 = 96,000 ($800 per month times 12 months times 10 units)

If you anticipate a 3% Vacancy and Credit Loss you will multiply as shown here to estimate a loss of $2,880:

96,000 x 0.03 = 2,880

Answer 7-3:

The total Gross Scheduled Income for the property is

900 x 12 x 8 = 86,400 ($900 per month x 12 months x 8 units)

If one unit was vacant for two months, you lost 900 x 2 or $1,800. Your vacancy percentage was 2.1%.

1,800 / 86,400 = 2.1%

Answer 7-4:

Of course, you took a one-month security deposit so you didn't lose anything. That should be the right answer but you want to practice your math, so pretend this was your spouse's distant cousin who said, "Trust me" and didn't give you a deposit. Don't make this harder than it needs to be. All the monthly rents are the same. You have six units, so in a year you have 6 x 12 or 72 months of potential rent. You lost one out of 72, which is one divided by 72, or 1.4%.

8

Gross Operating Income (Effective Gross Income)

Y ou know what you hope to collect: The Gross Scheduled Income. And you know that your hope will be tempered by the reality of Vacancy and Credit Loss. What is left – what you actually, realistically expect to collect before paying out any expenses, improvements or financing costs – is the Gross Operating Income, aka Effective Gross Income. The math is simple enough:

Gross Operating Income = Gross Scheduled Income less Vacancy and Credit Loss

An easier way to visualize this calculation is a "top down" approach as it might appear in a report or on a spreadsheet:

Gross Scheduled Income
less Vacancy and Credit Loss
= Gross Operating Income

Problem 8-1:

Your property's expected Gross Scheduled Income for next year is $38,000. You allow 3% for possible Vacancy and Credit Loss. What will your Gross Operating Income be?

Problem 8-2:

Your property's current Gross Scheduled Income is $50,000. You expect that amount to grow 2% in each of the next two years, 3% in the following two years, and 4% in the fifth year. You also expect your Vacancy and Credit Loss to be 3% each year. What is your projected Gross Operating Income for each of the next five years?

Answer 8-1:

Apply the formula.

Gross Operating Income = Gross Scheduled Income less Vacancy and Credit Loss.

Gross Operating Income = 38,000 less 3% of 38,000

Gross Operating Income = 38,000 less 1,140

Gross Operating Income = 36,860

Answer 8-2:

Although the problem asks you to figure out the Gross Operating Income for each of the next five years, you'll actually have to calculate the Gross Scheduled Income and the Vacancy and Credit Loss as well. Sneaky way to get you to practice compound interest and percents.

Start with the Gross Scheduled Income, which will grow 2% in each of the first two years, 3% in the following two years, and 4% in the fifth year. As you should recall from Chapter 2, compound interest is calculated with the formula Future Value = Principal x (1 + Periodic Rate) ^ Number of Periods. However, you have a series of five years involving three different interest rates and, in addition, you need to know to what amount your income grows each and every year. So the best approach is to take the compounding one year at a time.

In that case the exponent in the formula, ^Number of Periods, will be 1 in each step. As you recall from Algebra 1, which you may have experienced even before you read Chapter 2, any number with an exponent of 1 is simply itself, so you can forget about the exponent. Hence, the formula to step one period at a time is just Future Value = Principal x (1 + Periodic Rate). Let's determine the Gross Scheduled Income for each of the five years, rounded to the nearest dollar:

Year 1 GSI = 50,000 x 1.02 = 51,000

Year 2 GSI = 51,000 x 1.02 = 52,020

Year 3 GSI = 52,020 x 1.03 = 53,581

Year 4 GSI = 53,581 x 1.03 = 55,188

Year 5 GSI = 55,188 x 1.04 = 57,396

Next, you're ready to calculate the Vacancy and Credit Loss Allowance for each year:

51,000 x 0.03 = 1,530

52.020 x 0.03 = 1,561

53,581 x 0.03 = 1,607

55,188 x 0.03 = 1,656

57,396 x 0.03 = 1,722

Finally, subtract the Vacancy and Credit Loss from the Gross Scheduled Income and use the spreadsheet layout to display your results for each year:

	Year 1	Year 2	Year 3	Year 4	Year 5
Gross Scheduled Income	51,000	52,020	53,581	55,188	57,396
Less Vac. & Credit Loss	1,530	1,561	1,607	1,656	1,722
= Gross Operating Income	49,470	50,459	51,974	53,532	55,674

9

Net Operating Income

N et Operating Income (NOI) is what is left after you go one step further and reduce your Gross Operating Income by the total of all operating expenses.

Net Operating Income = Gross Operating Income less Operating Expenses

Again, you may find it easier to visualize this in a top-down format, as on a spreadsheet:

**Gross Operating Income
less Operating Expenses
= Net Operating Income**

Even more useful is to take it all the way from the top line, Gross Schedule Income.

**Gross Scheduled Income
less Vacancy and Credit Loss
= Gross Operating Income
less Operating Expenses
= Net Operating Income**

When doing this calculation, keep in mind that not all costs you may encounter qualify as operating expenses. You should not treat mortgage payments, depreciation, or capital improvements as operating expenses, even though they may, to some extent, be tax deductions. See this writer's book, *What Every Real Estate Investor Needs to Know About Cash Flow…*, for a more complete discussion.

Most experienced investors will use some variation of an "Annual Property Operating Data" or "APOD" form to work out their property's NOI. You can find a sample of such a form at www.realdata.com/book. You'll also see a trimmed-down version of the APOD in the solutions to the sample problems below.

Problem 9-1:

You operate an apartment building with six units that rent for $850 each per month, six that rent for $1,000 each, and six that rent for $1,200 each. The building is fully occupied but you estimate that you will lose 4% in the next year due to vacancy and credit losses. You project that you will have the following costs over the next 12 months:

Accounting	1,400
Advertising	2,000
Electricity	1,400
Insurance	4,750
Property Management	15,400
Real Estate Taxes	13,000
Repairs and Maintenance	8,500
Supplies	600
Trash Removal	2,400
Water	1,600

Build a form showing your expected income, vacancy allowance, operating expenses and Net Operating Income.

Problem 9-2:

You operate a mixed-use building with 12 apartments that rent for $2,000 each per month and four penthouse units that rent for $4,500 each. At street level you have 18,000 square feet of retail space. Half of that space rents for $52 per square foot per year, one-quarter for $58 per square foot, and the remainder for $62 per square foot. You estimate your potential vacancy and credit loss at 3% and project the following costs related to your ownership and operation of the property:

Accounting	2,200
Advertising	3,000
Depreciation Expense	160,000
Electricity	23,000
Improvements	82,000
Insurance	48,000
Legal	16,500
Mortgage Interest	220,000
Property Management	30,000
Real Estate Taxes	128,000
Repairs and Maintenance	92,000
Snow Removal	5,000
Supplies	8,800
Trash Removal	18,000
Water	14,200

Fill in an APOD form showing your expected income, vacancy allowance, operating expenses and Net Operating Income.

Answer 9-1:

First you need to calculate your Gross Schedule Income:

$850 x 12 months x 6 units = 61,200

$1,000 x 12 months x 6 units = 72,000

$1,200 x 12 months x 6 units = 86,400

Your total Gross Scheduled Income is $219,600

Next, figure your Vacancy and Credit Loss Allowance:

219,600 x 0.04 = 8,784

Subtract this amount from your Gross Scheduled Income for a GOI of $210,816. Finally, subtract your operating expenses, which total $51,050, and put everything into an APOD form to find your NOI of $159,766.

ANNUAL PROPERTY OPERATING DATA	
INCOME	
Gross Scheduled Rent Income	219,600
Other Income	0
TOTAL GROSS INCOME	219,600
VACANCY & CREDIT ALLOWANCE	8,784
GROSS OPERATING INCOME	210,816
EXPENSES	
Accounting	1,400
Advertising	2,000
Insurance (fire and liability)	4,750
Janitorial Service	0
Lawn/Snow	0
Legal	0
Licenses	0
Miscellaneous	0
Property Management	15,400
Repairs and Maintenance	8,500
Resident Superintendent	0
Supplies	600
Taxes	
Real Estate	13,000
Personal Property	0
Payroll	0
Other	0
Trash Removal	2,400
Utilities	
Electricity	1,400
Fuel Oil	0
Gas	0
Sewer and Water	1,600
Telephone	0
Other	0
TOTAL EXPENSES	51,050
NET OPERATING INCOME	159,766

Answer 9-2:

Again, begin by calculating the Gross Scheduled Income:

$2,000 x 12 months x 12 units = 288,000

$4,500 x 12 months x 4 units = 216,000

9,000 sf @ $52/sf = 468,000

4,500 sf @ $58/sf = 261,000

4,500 sf @ $62/sf = 279,000

Add these up to get your total Gross Scheduled Income of $1,512,000.

Next, figure your Vacancy and Credit Loss Allowance:

1,512,000 x 0.03 = 45,360

As in the previous problem, subtract this Vacancy and Credit Allowance from your Gross Scheduled Income. This leaves you with a GOI of $1,466,640. Finally, list your projected operating expenses, which total $388,700, and put everything into an APOD form to find your NOI of $1,077,940.

ANNUAL PROPERTY OPERATING DATA	
INCOME	
Gross Scheduled Rent Income	1,512,000
Other Income	0
TOTAL GROSS INCOME	1,512,000
VACANCY & CREDIT ALLOWANCE	45,360
GROSS OPERATING INCOME	1,466,640
EXPENSES	
Accounting	2,200
Advertising	3,000
Insurance (fire and liability)	48,000
Janitorial Service	0
Lawn/Snow	5,000
Legal	16,500
Licenses	0
Miscellaneous	0
Property Management	30,000
Repairs and Maintenance	92,000
Resident Superintendent	0
Supplies	8,800
Taxes	
Real Estate	128,000
Personal Property	0
Payroll	0
Other	0
Trash Removal	18,000
Utilities	
Electricity	23,000
Fuel Oil	0
Gas	0
Sewer and Water	14,200
Telephone	0
Other	0
TOTAL EXPENSES	388,700
NET OPERATING INCOME	1,077,940

Did you notice that not all of the so-called "costs" listed in the problem appear on the APOD? It's not a mistake. Depreciation, improvements and mortgage interest (as well as mortgage principal) are not operating expenses and don't belong here. Your mortgage interest, for example, may be deductible and will certainly lighten your wallet, but it's not necessary for the *operation* of the property so it's not an operating expense.

As you'll recall from my *Cash Flow* book, capitalization of the Net Operating Income is the most common way of estimating the value of income-producing real estate. If you distort the calculation of NOI by including in your APOD items that are not properly classified as expenses, then you're also going to distort your estimate of value. In this example, your inclusion of depreciation, improvements and mortgage interest would have dramatically reduced your property's supposed NOI and likewise any estimate of value you might have made using that bogus number.

10

Capitalization Rate

C apitalization Rate (or "cap rate") expresses the relationship between an income-property's value and its Net Operating Income. This writer admittedly made a big deal in the last chapter about getting the NOI right – about not contaminating the calculation with costs that weren't really operating expenses. That's because it is a big deal. If you compute the NOI incorrectly then much of what follows, including your estimate of value, will also be incorrect.

You calculate a property's simple or market capitalization rate as follows:

Capitalization Rate = Net Operating Income / Value

As a practical matter, the "value" here may be the price at which a property is offered, and your purpose is to perform the calculation to determine if the resulting cap rate meets your investment objectives. Or it may be the price at which the property was actually sold, and your purpose is to discover the cap rate (or rates) at which transactions in your market are occurring.

Often you will want to transpose this formula to estimate what a property is worth, given a required cap rate:

Value = Net Operating Income / Capitalization Rate

Occasionally you might want to see what a property's NOI would have to be in order to yield a given cap rate at a given price:

Net Operating Income = Value x Capitalization Rate

Problem 10-1:

A property has a Gross Scheduled Income of $100,000, a Vacancy and Credit Loss Allowance of 3%, and operating expenses of $34,000. What cap rate would you realize if you purchased the property for $600,000? For $800,000? For $1,000,000?

Problem 10-2:

You are considering the purchase of one of four income properties. The first has a NOI of $78,000 and is offered for sale at $760,000. The second has a NOI of $84,000 and is offered at $925,000. The third has a NOI of $72,000 and is offered at $650,000. The fourth has a NOI of $90,000 and is offered at $795,000. You're looking for a property with no less than an 11% cap rate. Which if any of these properties meets your criterion? For the properties that do not, at what price would they yield 11%?

Problem 10-3:

You had a dream that all of the other people in your investment club would laugh at you behind your back if you settled for less than a 12% cap rate. At what price would have to buy each of the properties in Problem 10-2 to satisfy that requirement and get a good night's sleep?

Problem 10-4:

You meet someone at your yoga class who intrudes on your serenity and tries to sell you an office building. He wants $3 million for the property and boasts that the lucky buyer will be getting it at a 10% cap rate. You fan away his cigar smoke, then shift the focus of your meditation to calculating mentally the Net

Operating Income that would be necessary to achieve a 10% cap rate at his asking price. What is that NOI?

Answer 10-1:

You begin by calculating the property's Net Operating Income. Use this formula from Chapter 9:

> Gross Scheduled Income
> less Vacancy and Credit Loss
> = Gross Operating Income
> less Operating Expenses
> = Net Operating Income

> 100,000 Gross Scheduled Income
> less 3% of 100,000, or 3,000 Vacancy and Credit
> = 97,000 Gross Operating Income
> less 34,000 Expenses
> = 63,000 Net Operating Income

Now you can apply the formula above for capitalization rate, using each of the three values specified in the problem.

> Capitalization Rate = Net Operating Income / Value

> Capitalization Rate = 63,000 / 600,000

> Capitalization Rate = 10.5%

> Capitalization Rate = 63,000 / 800,000

> Capitalization Rate = 7.875%

> Capitalization Rate = 63,000 / 1,000,000

> Capitalization Rate = 6.3%

Answer 10-2:

Again, apply the formula for capitalization rate to each of the four properties:

Capitalization Rate = Net Operating Income / Value

Capitalization Rate = 78,000 / 760,000   (Property 1)

Capitalization Rate = 10.27%

Capitalization Rate = 84,000 / 925,000   (Property 2)

Capitalization Rate = 9.08%

Capitalization Rate = 72,000 / 650,000   (Property 3)

Capitalization Rate = 11.08%

Capitalization Rate = 90,000 / 795,000   (Property 4)

Capitalization Rate = 11.32%

Properties 3 and 4 meet your 11% criterion. To calculate the price at which Properties 1 and 2 would yield 11%, use this formula:

Value = Net Operating Income / Capitalization Rate

Value = 78,000 / 0.11   (Property 1)

Value = 709,091

Value = 84,000 / 0.11   (Property 2)

Value = 763,636

Answer 10-3:

To find the price (i.e., the value) at which each of the properties in Problem 10-2 would yield a 12% capitalization rate, you use exactly the same procedure as in the second half of that problem.

Value = Net Operating Income / Capitalization Rate

Value = 78,000 / 0.12   (Property 1)

Value = 650,000

Value = 84,000 / 0.12   (Property 2)

Value = 700,000

Value = 72,000 / 0.12   (Property 3)

Value = 600,000

Value = 90,000 / 0.12   (Property 4)

Value = 750,000

Answer 10-4:

The formula you need is Net Operating Income = Value x Capitalization Rate. You can remain in your lotus position and do this in your head.

Net Operating Income = Value x Capitalization Rate

Net Operating Income = $3 million x 10%

Net Operating Income = $300,000

11

Net Income Multiplier

T he Net Income Multiplier (NIM) is simply the reciprocal of the capitalization rate:

Net Income Multiplier = 1 / Capitalization Rate

Its purpose is to serve as a convenience for those occasions, as in the previous problem, where you may have to do some math in your head. Most people find hands-free multiplication easier than division, so if you know that the prevailing cap rate in your market is 9%, 10%, 11% or whatever, you can find the reciprocal, round it off, and have it ready to use if the need should arise.

For example, with a 9% cap rate the equivalent Net Income Multiplier = 1 / 0.09 or 11.1. For a 10% cap rate, the equivalent NIM = 1 / 0.10 or 10. And for an 11% cap it is 1 / 0.11 or 9.09.

You could round those off and use 11, 10, or 9, respectively, to do the math in your head.

Your purpose is essentially the same as with a cap rate, to estimate the value of a property when you know its NOI.

Value = Net Income Multiplier x Net Operating Income

Problem 11-1:

The current prevailing cap rate in your market is 9%. Someone standing next to you on the subway asks if you would like to by a building with a NOI of $1 million. You say, "Of course" and start to write a check. Use the rounded NIM to estimate the building's value. Don't use a pencil to solve the problem, or when writing the check. Also, don't buy a Rolex from this person.

Problem 11-2:

The current prevailing cap rate in your market is 11%. Someone mentions a nice property with a NOI of $150,000. You can't do that value calculation in your head. Or can you?

Answer 11-1:

A 9% cap rate is equivalent to a Net Income Multiplier of approximately 11. If the property's NOI is $1 million, you would estimate its value at about $11 million.

Value = Net Income Multiplier x Net Operating Income

Value = 11 x 1,000,000

Value = 11,000,000

Answer 11-2:

An 11% cap rate is equivalent to a Net Income Multiplier of approximately 9.

Don't be embarrassed that you can't multiply 9 x 150,000 in your head. But you definitely can handle 10 x 150,000, which is 1.5 million. Ten "150,000s" is one more than nine "150,000s," so you need to knock off 150,000 from your 1.5 million to get the answer you need, and that's easy to do without a pencil: $1,350,000.

12

Taxable Income

The calculation of a real estate investment's taxable income does not follow any law of nature or mathematics, but rather the sometimes unnatural law of the U.S. tax code. Whatever the tax code says is income, is income; whatever the code says is a deduction, is a deduction. The difference between the two is the taxable income. Fortunately, the definitions of income and deduction haven't changed much in recent history, so the principles stated here are likely still to be correct when you read them.

The following top-down formula will lead to the taxable income:

Gross Scheduled Income
less Vacancy and Credit Loss
= Gross Operating Income
less Operating Expenses
= Net Operating Income
less Mortgage Interest
less Depreciation, Real Property
less Depreciation, Capital Additions (Improvements)
less Amortization of Points and Closing Costs
plus Interest Earned
= Taxable Income

Keep in mind that you may depreciate only the physical structures, not the land, and that the length over which you take this write-off currently depends on whether the property is residential or non-residential (as of this writing 27.5 and 39 years, respectively). You generally write off closing costs for investment property over the same number of years as the building. "Points" paid to secure financing are typically deducted over the term of the loan. "Interest Earned" commonly refers to interest on property bank accounts.

Problem 12-1:

You have a small retail property with a current-year Net Operating Income of $100,000. When you purchased it several years ago, you paid closing costs of $5,000 and one loan point on a $600,000, 20-year mortgage. You paid $38,000 in interest on the mortgage this year. The value of the building (excluding the land) at the time of purchase was $800,000. During your first year of ownership, you made capital improvements costing $195,000. You earned $27 interest on your property's checking account this year. What is your taxable income for the year?

Problem 12-2:

You have an office building from which you collected $180,000 in Gross Operating Income this year. Your operating expenses were $62,000 and the interest on your mortgage was $41,000. You paid two points to get that $800,000 loan last year. It was a 15-year mortgage with a five-year balloon. You bought the property for $1.3 million, at which time the tax assessor's appraised value for the building was $770,000, and $330,000 for the land. Your closing costs were $8,000. Last year you made $50,000 in capital improvements. This year you earned $34 in interest on your bank account. What is your taxable income for the current year?

Answer 12 -1:

Because you've been given the Net Operating Income, you can start applying the formula from that point:

Net Operating Income
less Mortgage Interest
less Depreciation, Real Property
less Depreciation, Capital Additions (Improvements)
less Amortization of Points and Closing Costs
plus Interest Earned
= Taxable Income

The problem specifies some of the items, but leaves others for you to figure out. Begin by filling in the items you know:

100,000 (Net Operating Income)
less 38,000 (Mortgage Interest)
less Depreciation, Real Property
less Depreciation, Capital Additions (Improvements)
less Amortization of Points and Closing Costs
plus 27 (Interest Earned)
= Taxable Income

To calculate the depreciation on the real property, take the value of improvements at the time of purchase and divide it by the useful life under the current tax code for non-residential real estate:

800,000 / 39 = 20,513

Note that the problem specifies you purchased the property several years ago. If you had purchased it this year, you would have had to pro-rate the depreciation according to the number of months the property was in service, and also excluded half of the first month. Why? Because those are the rules according to the current tax code.

You calculate the depreciation on capital additions in the same was as you did with the building.

195,000 / 39 = 5,000

Next, calculate the deductible portion of your closing costs by dividing the total amount by the useful life of the property:

5,000 / 39 = 128

Finally you need to determine what portion of your loan points can be deducted this year. You paid one point on a $600,000, 20-year mortgage. One percent of $600,000 is $6,000; divide that by 20 years to get the amount to deduct in a full year:

6,000 / 20 = 300

Now you can fill in the rest of the formula.

100,000 (Net Operating Income)
less 38,000 (Mortgage Interest)
less 20,513 (Depreciation, Real Property)
less 5,000 (Depreciation, Capital Additions)
less 300 (Amortization of Points) and 128 (Closing Costs)
plus 27 (Interest Earned)
= Taxable Income

With just the numbers, for clarity:

100,000
less 38,000
less 20,513
less 5,000
less (300 + 128)
plus 27
= 36,086

Your taxable income is $36,086.

Answer 12-2:

Because you've been given the Gross Operating Income, you can start applying the formula from that point:

Gross Operating Income
less Operating Expenses
= Net Operating Income
less Mortgage Interest

less Depreciation, Real Property
less Depreciation, Capital Additions (Improvements)
less Amortization of Points and Closing Costs
plus Interest Earned
= Taxable Income

Like the previous problem this one specifies some of the items, but leaves others for you to figure out. Begin be filling in the items you know:

180,000 (Gross Operating Income)
less 62,000 (Operating Expenses)
= (Net Operating Income)
less 41,000 (Mortgage Interest)
less Depreciation, Real Property
less Depreciation, Capital Additions (Improvements)
less Amortization of Points and Closing Costs
plus 34 (Interest Earned)
= Taxable Income

The Net Operating Income requires just simple subtraction:

180,000 less 62,000

to give you the correct amount, $118,000.

To calculate the depreciation on the real property, you first need to make a reasonable estimate as to what portion of the value of the entire property lies in the buildings. Note that the tax assessor appraised the building at $770,000. Is that the number you should use? Probably not, since that appraisal could have been made several years ago. A more defensible approach is to take the assessor's building appraisal and compare that the appraised value of the property as a whole – in other words, find the ratio of the building appraisal to the whole. The building appraisal is $770,000 and the whole property is the land plus the building, i.e., $330,000 plus $770,000, or $1.1 million. The ratio of the building to the whole then is 70%

770,000 / 1,100,000 = 70%.

You paid $1.3 million for the property, so it is fair to say that the building, at the time of purchase, was worth 70% of that amount, or $910,000.

0.70 x 1,300,000 = 910,000

Since this is non-residential property, you will be writing it off over 39 years. Because you purchased it last year, you're allowed a full year of depreciation this year. Your depreciation deduction for the current year, therefore is $23,333.

910,000 / 39 = 23,333

Last year you made capital improvements of $50,000, so you are also entitled to a full year of depreciation on those.

50,000 / 39 = 1,282

Finally you need to calculate the amortization of loan points and closing costs. For the latter, you use the same useful life as the building and improvements. This year you can write off $205 of your $8,000 closing costs.

8,000 / 39 = 205

You paid two points, or $16,000, to get the $800,000 mortgage loan.

0.02 x 800,000 = 16,000

That amount couldn't be deducted all at once last year when you made your investment, but rather must be amortized over the term of the loan. Sorry, this was a trick question. It was a 15-year mortgage with a five-year balloon. Since you are obligated to pay the loan off in five years, you amortize the points over that period of time because that's when the debt really is supposed to mature, provided you don't skip the country. Your amortization of points is $3,200.

16,000 / 5 = 3,200

Now you can plug in these new values to complete your formula:

    180,000 (Gross Operating Income)
    less 62,000 (Operating Expenses)
    = 118,000 (Net Operating Income)
    less 41,000 (Mortgage Interest)
    less 23,333 (Depreciation, Real Property)

less 1,282 (Depreciation, Capital Additions)
less 3,200 (Amortization of Points) and 205 (Closing Costs)
plus 34 (Interest Earned)
= Taxable Income

Now with just the numbers:

180,000
less 62,000
= 118,000
less 41,000
less 23,333
less 1,282
less (3,200 + 205)
plus 34
= 49,014

Your taxable income is $49,014.

13

Cash Flow

L   ike the taxable income of the previous section, cash flow starts with Gross Scheduled Income, less Vacancy and Credit Loss, less Operating Expenses, which of course you know is another way of saying that it starts with Net Operating Income.

Unlike taxable income, however, the components of cash flow are unrelated to any tax implications. Cash flow is simply the net of all of a property's cash inflows less all of its cash outflows.

The top-down formula for cash flow looks like this:

Gross Scheduled Income
less Vacancy and Credit Loss
= Gross Operating Income
less Operating Expenses
= Net Operating Income
less Debt Service
less Capital Additions (Improvements)
plus Loan Proceeds
plus Interest Earned
= Cash Flow Before Taxes

Mortgage payments highlight one very obvious distinction between taxable income and cash flow. With taxable income, you're concerned only about the interest portion of the payment because that's the only part with tax implications – the interest typically is deductable. With cash flow, you care about the entire payment amount, because it is all a cash outflow.

The depreciation allowance is another big difference. You can deduct depreciation; therefore it affects your taxable income. It is not a cash item, so it has no affect on your cash flow – at least not on your cash flow before taxes.

If you can make a reasonable estimate of the tax liability generated by your ownership of a particular property – the simplest way being to take the taxable income and multiply it by your marginal tax bracket (the rate at which your next dollar of income will be taxed) – you can then subtract that tax liability to get your Cash Flow After Taxes.

Cash Flow Before Taxes
less Tax Liability
= Cash Flow After Taxes

Problem 13-1:

You have a property, with 10 rental units at $1,000 per month and 10 at $1,200 per month. You anticipate a 3% loss due to vacancy and credit. Your operating expenses average $5,500 per month. You have a mortgage with a monthly payment of $6,800. You earn $250 for the year on your property's reserve-fund bank account. What is your property's cash flow this year?

Problem 13-2:

You have a property with an annual Net Operating Income of $67,500. The monthly payment on your first mortgage is $2,800. You have a second mortgage of $180,000 that is interest-only at 9% per year. What is your cash flow?

Problem 13-3:

You have a 5-unit property with annual debt service of $36,300 and annual operating expenses of $21,000. Assuming an average vacancy and credit loss of 3%, what average rent must you charge per unit in order to achieve a positive cash flow?

Problem 13-4:

Take the same property and facts as in Problem 13-1. In addition, you know that the property's taxable income is $95,000. Your marginal tax rate is 28%. Estimate the after-tax cash flow for this property.

Answer 13-1:

Start with your top-down formula:

Gross Scheduled Income
less Vacancy and Credit Loss
= Gross Operating Income
less Operating Expenses
= Net Operating Income
less Debt Service
less Capital Additions (Improvements)
plus Loan Proceeds
plus Interest Earned
= Cash Flow Before Taxes

Now begin filling in the lines as needed. Calculate the Gross Scheduled Income as follows:

(10 units x 1,000 per mo. x 12 months) + (10 units x 1,200 per mo. x 12 months)

Gross Scheduled Income = 120,000 + 144,000

Gross Scheduled Income = 264,000

From that, calculate the Vacancy and Credit Loss of 3%:

Vacancy and Credit Loss = 264,000 x 0.03

Vacancy and Credit Loss = 7,920

Next, the Gross Operating Income:

264,000 (Gross Scheduled Income)
less 7,920 (Vacancy and Credit Loss)
= 256,080 (Gross Operating Income)

Your operating expenses average $5,500 per month, so multiply that by 12 for annual expenses of $66,000. Your mortgage payment is $6,800 per month; times 12 equals $81,600 per year. Your interest earned for the year is $250.

You now have enough information to fill in the formula:

264,000 (Gross Scheduled Income)
less 7,920 (Vacancy and Credit Loss)
= 256,080 (Gross Operating Income)
less 66,000 (Operating Expenses)
= 190,080 (Net Operating Income)
less 81,600 (Debt Service)
less 0 (Capital Additions (Improvements))
plus 0 (Loan Proceeds)
plus 250 (Interest Earned)
= 108,730 (Cash Flow Before Taxes)

Your cash flow before taxes for the year is $108,730.

Answer 13-2:

You can compact the formula quite a bit here because the problem starts you off at the Net Operating Income of $67,500, from which you need to subtract the only other relevant item, the annual debt service. In this case, however, there are two mortgages, so you need to find the debt service for each, then combine those amounts.

The first mortgage has monthly payments of $2,800, so the annual debt service for that loan is $33,600.

The second mortgage of $180,000 has payments that are interest-only at 9% per year.

$$180,000 \times 0.09 = 16,200$$

Would the result be any different if you presumed monthly payments? The monthly rate would be $1/12^{th}$ of 9%, or 0.0075.

$$180,000 \times 0.0075 \times 12 \text{ months} = 16,200$$

The total annual debt service is 33,600 plus 16,200, or 49,800.

Now you can calculate the cash flow.

> 67,500 (Net Operating Income)
> less 49,800 (Debt Service)
> = 17,700 (Cash Flow Before Taxes)

Answer 13-3:

This is not really a trick question. You'll use the same cash flow formula, but you'll solve for the Gross Scheduled Income instead. You can do this either by working the top-down approach backwards, or by transposing the formula algebraically. We'll demonstrate both ways.

Let's start with the standard formula, omitting the variables that are not pertinent to the example: improvements, loan proceeds and interest earned.

> Gross Scheduled Income
> less Vacancy and Credit Loss
> = Gross Operating Income
> less Operating Expenses
> = Net Operating Income
> less Debt Service
> = Cash Flow Before Taxes

Work from the bottom up instead of top down. For simplicity, say that you're looking for the rent that will give you a zero cash flow. Once you've found that, you can then say that any rent greater than that amount will give you a positive cash flow.

So, from the bottom, look at this segment:

    = Net Operating Income
    less Debt Service
    = Cash Flow Before Taxes

You know that your annual debt service is $36,300. What NOI do you need to yield a cash flow of zero? Clearly, it must be the same, $36,300.

    = 36,300 (Net Operating Income)
    less 36,300 (Debt Service)
    = 0 (Cash Flow Before Taxes)

You were given operating expenses of $21,000, and you now know your NOI is $36,300. Climb the ladder another rung.

    = Gross Operating Income
    less 21,000 (Operating Expenses)
    = 36,300 (Net Operating Income)

Since the NOI is the difference, the GOI must be the sum, $57,300.

    = 57,300 (Gross Operating Income)
    less 21,000 (Operating Expenses)
    = 36,300 (Net Operating Income)

You're almost there. What Gross Scheduled Income, less 3% vacancy loss, would give you $57,300? In other words, 57,300 is 97% of what number?

    57,300 / 0.97 = 59,072

Test to see if it's true;

    59,072 (Gross Scheduled Income) x 0.03 = 1,772 (Vacancy and Credit Loss)

59,072 less 1,772 = 57,300 Gross Operating Income

Your final mathematical backflip is to calculate the average monthly rent per unit.

59,072 / 12 = 4,922.67, the total month rent

4922.67 / 5 units = 984.53 per unit

Since, this number yields a zero cash flow, anything above this amount – say $985 – would yield a positive cash flow

Those readers who are not algebraically challenged will realize that they could have taken the basic formula and transposed it to solve directly for a different variable. Start with:

Cash Flow Before Taxes = Gross Scheduled Income less Vacancy and Credit Loss less Operating Expenses less Debt Service

(Note: It's ok to omit "= Gross Operating Income" and "= Net Operating Income" from the original formula because those are just subtotals.)

Then express the Vacancy in terms of Gross Scheduled Income:

Cash Flow Before Taxes = Gross Scheduled Income less 3% of Gross Scheduled Income less Operating Expenses less Debt Service or,

Cash Flow Before Taxes = (0.97 x Gross Scheduled Income) less Operating Expenses less Debt Service

Now transpose the formula:

Cash Flow Before Taxes plus Operating Expenses plus Debt Service = 0.97 x Gross Scheduled Income

Divide both sides by 0.97:

(Cash Flow Before Taxes plus Operating Expenses plus Debt Service) / 0.97 = Gross Scheduled Income

Now try it, remembering that you're looking for the Gross Scheduled Income that corresponds to a zero cash flow:

(0 + 21,000 + 36,300) / 0.97

57,300 / 0.97 = 59,072

By transposing the formula, you directly calculated the same Gross Scheduled Income as you did with the previous approach.

Answer 13-4:

In order to answer this question, you must have first answered Problem 13-1 correctly. If you did, then you know that its cash flow before taxes is $108,730.

Next you need to estimate your tax liability. The problem states that the property's taxable income is $95,000, and your marginal tax bracket is 28%. Hence, a reasonable estimate of your tax liability from this property is $26,600.

95,000 x 0.28 = 26,600

Apply the formula

    Cash Flow Before Taxes
    less Tax Liability
    = Cash Flow After Taxes

    108,730 (Cash Flow Before Taxes)
    less 26,600 (Tax Liability)
    = 82,130 (Cash Flow After Taxes)

Your estimated Cash Flow After Taxes is $82,130.

14

Cash-on-Cash Return

C ash-on-Cash Return, also known as the Equity Dividend Rate, is a measure of investment return expressed as the ratio between the cash flow (typically before taxes) and initial cash investment. It gives no weight to the time value of money, so it is most meaningful if used with the first-year's cash flow. In other words, the more time that elapses between the initial investment and the cash flow being measured, the less meaningful the relationship between the two.

Cash-on-Cash Return = Annual Cash Flow / Cash Invested

Problem 14-1:

You invest $70,000 in a property whose first year Cash Flow Before Taxes is $5,600. What is the property's Cash-on-Cash return that year?

Problem 14-2:

You purchase a property for $400,000 with a $320,000 first mortgage. It has a Net Operating Income of $37,000. The monthly mortgage payment is $2,417. What is the property's first-year Cash-on-Cash Return?

Problem 14-3:

You purchase a property for $600,000 with a $480,000 first mortgage. It has a Gross Operating Income of $95,000 and operating expenses of $37,500. The monthly mortgage payment is $3,547. What is the property's first-year Cash-on-Cash Return?

Problem 14-4:

With the property in Problem 14-3, the seller agrees to take a purchase-money note for $100,000, interest-only at 7% for seven years. Now what is the Cash-on Cash return? What happens if the seller takes back $120,000?

Answer 14-1:

Apply the formula,

Cash-on-Cash Return = Annual Cash Flow / Cash Invested

Cash-on-Cash Return = 5,600 / 70,000

Cash-on-Cash Return = 8%

Answer 14-2:

First you need to calculate both the cash flow and the initial investment amount. Extracting just the portion of the cash flow formula from the previous chapter that is needed here, you subtract the debt service from the NOI to figure the cash flow:

Net Operating Income
less Debt Service
= Cash Flow Before Taxes

37,000 (Net Operating Income)
less 29,004 (2,417 x 12 Debt Service)
= 7,996 Cash Flow Before Taxes

Next find the initial investment, which is the difference between the purchase price and the financing amount:

400,000 (Purchase Price)
less 320,000 (Mortgage Financing)
= 80,000 (Cash Invested)

Apply the formula

Cash-on-Cash Return = Annual Cash Flow / Cash Invested

Cash-on-Cash Return = 7,996 / 80,000

Cash-on-Cash Return = 10%

Answer 14-3:

Your approach is basically the same as in the previous problem except that you will need to use a slightly larger chunk of the cash flow formula:

Gross Operating Income
less Operating Expenses
= Net Operating Income
less Debt Service
= Cash Flow Before Taxes

Now plug in the facts you know to determine the cash flow:

95,000 (Gross Operating Income)
less 37,500 (Operating Expenses)
= 57,500 (Net Operating Income)
less 42,564 (3,547 x 12 Debt Service)
= 14,936 (Cash Flow Before Taxes)

Next find the initial investment, which is the difference between the purchase price and the financing amount:

600,000 (Purchase Price)
less 480,000 (Mortgage Financing)
= 120,000 (Cash Invested)

Apply the formula:

Cash-on-Cash Return = Annual Cash Flow / Cash Invested

Cash-on-Cash Return = 14,936 / 120,000

Cash-on-Cash Return = 12.45%

Answer 14-4:

The additional financing will have an effect on two aspects of your cash-on-cash calculation: the cash flow and the amount of cash invested.

To account for the cash flow impact, take your previous calculation and add another debt service row. The annual interest-only payment on $100,000 at 7% is $7,000. Note that the seven-year term is irrelevant, because you are looking at the first year only.

95,000 (Gross Operating Income)
less 37,500 (Operating Expenses)
= 57,500 (Net Operating Income)
less 42,564 (3,547 x 12 Debt Service)
less 7,000 (100,000 x 0.07 Interest-Only Purchase Money Note)
= 7,936 (Cash Flow Before Taxes)

Now recalculate the initial investment:

600,000 (Purchase Price)
less 480,000 (First Mortgage)
less 100,000 (Purchase Money Note)
= 20,000 (Cash Invested)

Apply the formula

Cash-on-Cash Return = Annual Cash Flow / Cash Invested

Cash-on-Cash Return = 7,936 / 20,000

Cash-on-Cash Return = 39.68%

What happens if the seller takes back $120,000? Don't even bother with the cash flow calculation; look again at the formula:

Cash-on-Cash Return = Annual Cash Flow / Cash Invested

If the seller takes back $120,000, then the sum of your two mortgages will equal the purchase price. In other words, your cash invested will be zero. Now think back to that high-school algebra class. What is any number divided by zero? Infinity. So, even a penny of cash flow represents an infinite return on investment.

To put this in less abstract terms, if you don't have any skin in the game it makes no sense to try to measure your cash-on-cash or any other kind of return. With nothing at risk you have no investment and so any attempt to calculate a return on investment is essentially meaningless.

15

Sale Proceeds

Your ongoing cash flows occur year-to-year as you operate a property. However, there is what you might call a special-case cash flow that occurs just once, when you sell the property. That cash flow is called the Sale Proceeds.

Typically there are three components in the calculation of the Sale Proceeds. First, of course, is the selling price itself. There are also the Costs of Sale, which include items such as brokerage commissions and legal fees. Finally, there is the payment of any outstanding mortgage balances.

Selling Price
less Costs of Sale
less Mortgage Payoff
= Sale Proceeds Before Taxes

As with operating cash flows, the Sales Proceeds are likely to incur a tax liability. Unlike operating cash flow, the tax due at the time of sale will almost certainly be subject to a complex string of calculations, not a simple percentage. Still the proceeds after tax are expressed simply as

Sale Proceeds Before Taxes
less Tax on Sale
= Sale Proceeds After Taxes

Problem 15-1:

You are selling a property for $500,000. The broker who handles the transaction charges you a commission of 5%. Your attorney charges you $4,250 in fees to close the sale. You owe the bank $315,000 on your mortgage. What proceeds can you expect to receive from the sale of the property?

Problem 15-2:

You are contemplating the sale of your investment property. Its current Net Operating Income is $40,000. Based on your market research, you believe it should sell at a capitalization rate between 8.5% and 9.5%. The broker you want to engage to handle the sale requires a commission of 5.5%. Your attorney quotes a flat fee of $5,000. You owe $285,000 on your mortgage. What sale proceeds do you expect to receive if you sell?

Problem 15-3:

The property you are selling shows a Gross Operating Income of $77,000, along with operating expenses of $21,000. You are confident that you can sell at a 9% capitalization rate. You expect to pay a brokerage commission of 6% and legal fees of $5,000. You'll need to pay off a mortgage of $390,000. Your accountant advises that you should expect to incur a tax liability of $19,500 on the sale. What do you expect to receive as before-tax and after-tax proceeds from this sale?

Answer 15-1:

First calculate your total Costs of Sale. A 5% commission on a $500,000 sale is $25,000. Add to this the $4,250 in legal fees for a total of $29,250.

Then apply the formula

> Selling Price
> less Costs of Sale
> less Mortgage Payoff
> = Sale Proceeds Before Taxes

Insert your data to find that your proceeds will be $155,750.

    500,000 (Selling Price)
    less 29,250 (Costs of Sale)
    less 315,000 (Mortgage Payoff)
    = 155,750 (Sale Proceeds Before Taxes)

Answer 15-2:

In this problem you need to calculate the selling price by capitalizing the Net Operating Income. Because you're given a range of cap rates, you'll have a range of potential selling prices and therefore a range of potential sales proceeds.

Start with the higher cap rate, which will give you the lower selling price. Apply the formula from Chapter 10:

Value = Net Operating Income / Capitalization Rate

Value = 40,000 / 0.095

Value = 421,053

Now find the total Costs of Sale. A 5.5% commission on a selling price of $421,053 is $23,158. Add $5,000 in legal fees for total Costs of Sale of $28,158.

Now apply the formula for Sale Proceeds:

    Selling Price
    less Costs of Sale
    less Mortgage Payoff
    = Sale Proceeds Before Taxes

Fill in the data to find Sale Proceeds of $107,895:

    421,053 (Selling Price)
    less 28,158 (Costs of Sale)
    less 285,000 (Mortgage Payoff)
    = 107,895 (Sale Proceeds Before Taxes)

Repeat this procedure with the lower cap rate, which will give you the higher end of the sales price range.

Value = Net Operating Income / Capitalization Rate

Value = 40,000 / 0.085

Value = 470,588

Now find the total Costs of Sale. A 5.5% commission on a selling price of $470,588 is $25,882. Add $5,000 in legal fees for total Costs of Sale of $30,882.

Again, apply the formula for Sale Proceeds:

Selling Price
less Costs of Sale
less Mortgage Payoff
= Sale Proceeds Before Taxes

Fill in the data to find Sale Proceeds of $154,706:

470,588 (Selling Price)
less 30,882 (Costs of Sale)
less 285,000 (Mortgage Payoff)
= 154,706 (Sale Proceeds Before Taxes)

Depending on the cap rate you actually achieve, you can expect Sale Proceeds to be between $107,895 and $154,706.

Answer 15-3:

In this problem you need to do just a little extra work to determine the selling price; and you can also go one step further to estimate the Sale Proceeds After Taxes.

Start by taking what you learned in Chapter 9 and determining the property's NOI:

Gross Operating Income
less Operating Expenses
= Net Operating Income

Insert the data to find the NOI:

77,000   (Gross Operating Income)
less 21,000 (Operating Expenses)
= 56,000 (Net Operating Income)

Then use the formula from Chapter 10 to estimate value:

Value = Net Operating Income / Capitalization Rate

Value = 56,000 / 0.09

Value = 622,222

Calculate the total Costs of Sale. A 6% commission on a selling price of $622,222 is $37,333. Add to this amount your legal fees of $5,000 for total Costs of Sale of $42,333.

As in the previous problems, apply the formula for Sale Proceeds:

Selling Price
less Costs of Sale
less Mortgage Payoff
= Sale Proceeds Before Taxes

Fill in the data to find Sale Proceeds of $189,889:

622,222 (Selling Price)
less 42,333 (Costs of Sale)
less 390,000 (Mortgage Payoff)
= 189,889 (Sale Proceeds Before Taxes)

Finally, figure your Sales Proceeds After Taxes:
Sale Proceeds Before Taxes
less Tax on Sale
= Sale Proceeds After Taxes

Fill in the tax liability to find the after-tax amount of $170,389:

189,889 (Sale Proceeds Before Taxes)
less 19,500 (Tax on Sale)
= 170,389 (Sale Proceeds After Taxes)

16

Discounted Cash Flow

T he good news is, you already know how to calculate Discounted Cash Flow (DCF) – assuming, of course, you didn't start reading this book from the middle. Go back to Chapter 4, Present Value, and have a quick review. In that chapter you learned how to find the Present Value of a single cash flow. With a real estate investment, unless you hold it for a very short time, you expect not just one cash flow but rather a series of them. As you saw in Chapters 13 and 15, you expect to receive cash flows each year you operate a property and also a one-time cash flow when you sell.

With Discounted Cash Flow, you perform a Present Value calculation on each of the cash flows in the series. When you have figured out the Present Value of each future cash flow, you add the PVs up and that number represents the Present Value of the entire income stream.

You can accomplish this manually, by looking up the PV factor for the rate and period of time:

Annual Present Value Factors

Years	9.875%	10.000%	10.125%	10.250%	10.375%	10.500%	10.625%	10.750%
1	0.910125	0.909091	0.908059	0.907029	0.906002	0.904977	0.903955	0.902935
2	0.828328	0.826446	0.824571	0.822702	0.820840	0.818984	0.817134	0.815291
3	0.753882	0.751315	0.748759	0.746215	0.743683	0.741162	0.738652	0.736154
4	0.686127	0.683013	0.679918	0.676839	0.673778	0.670735	0.667708	0.664699
5	0.624461	0.620921	0.617405	0.613913	0.610445	0.607000	0.603578	0.600180
6	0.568338	0.564474	0.560641	0.556837	0.553064	0.549321	0.545607	0.541923
7	0.517259	0.513158	0.509095	0.505068	0.501078	0.497123	0.493204	0.489321
8	0.470770	0.466507	0.462288	0.458112	0.453977	0.449885	0.445835	0.441825

Or you can use a simple Excel model to perform the calculation. Downloads of both the table and the model are available at http://www.realdata.com/book.

To do this with the table of factors, it will help if you have some sort of form to organize your information. The one below should work. In the first column of figures, list your cash flows. In the second, specify the discount rate at the top, then fill in the factor for each intersection of rate and years. Multiply the cash flow by the factor to fill in the PV column, then add up the PVs to determine the entire Discounted Cash Flow.

	Factor @ x%	PV
Cash Flow, End of Year 1	0 0	0
Cash Flow, End of Year 2	0 0	0
Cash Flow, End of Year 3	0 0	0
Cash Flow, End of Year 4	0 0	0
Cash Flow, End of Year 5	0 0	0
Cash Flow, End of Year 6	0 0	0
Cash Flow, End of Year 7	0 0	0
Cash Flow, End of Year 8	0 0	0
Cash Flow, End of Year 9	0 0	0
Cash Flow, End of Year 10	0 0	0
TOTAL PV		0

Problem 16-1:

You estimate the following cash flows from your property over the next seven years:

Year 1:	1,712
Year 2:	2,348
Year 3:	3,777
Year 4:	4,228
Year 5:	4,998
Year 6:	5,863
Year 7:	6,775

You also expect to sell the property at the end of Year 7 and realize cash proceeds of $185,000. You believe that the appropriate discount rate for your market is 10.5%. Perform a Discounted Cash Flow Analysis to determine the Present Value of this stream of future cash flows.

Problem 16-2:

You estimate the following cash flows from your property over the next seven years:

Year 1:	3,899
Year 2:	6,244
Year 3:	3,111
Year 4:	4,885
Year 5:	7,362
Year 6:	5,905
Year 7:	8,344

You also expect to sell the property at the end of Year 7 for $475,000. It will cost you a 5% broker's commission to do so, as well as $4,500 in legal fees. You will also have to pay off a mortgage of $267,000. You believe that the appropriate discount rate for your market is 10%. Perform a Discounted Cash Flow Analysis to determine the Present Value of this stream of future cash flows.

Answer 16-1:

You will need to fill in the form in order to find and then sum the Present Values. Start by entering the cash flows. Remember that you must add the operating cash flow and the sale proceeds for Year 7.

Then look up the PV factor for each year under the 10.5% discount column. Multiply each cash flow by its corresponding factor to determine its PV, then add up the PVs.

	Factor @ 10.5%	PV
Cash Flow, End of Year 1	1,712	0.904977	1,549.32
Cash Flow, End of Year 2	2,348	0.818984	1,922.97
Cash Flow, End of Year 3	3,777	0.741162	2,799.37
Cash Flow, End of Year 4	4,228	0.670735	2,835.87
Cash Flow, End of Year 5	4,998	0.607000	3,033.79
Cash Flow, End of Year 6	5,863	0.549321	3,220.67
Cash Flow, End of Year 7	191,775	0.497123	95,335.76
Cash Flow, End of Year 8	0	0	0
Cash Flow, End of Year 9	0	0	0
Cash Flow, End of Year 10	0	0	0
TOTAL PV			110,697.75

The Present Value of this series of cash flows to the nearest dollar is $110,698.

Answer 16-2:

Again you will need to fill in the form in order to find and then sum the Present Values. Start by entering the cash flows. You must add the operating cash flow and the sale proceeds for Year 7, but before you can do that you'll need to figure out the sale proceeds. Apply the formula from Chapter 15:

Selling Price
less Costs of Sale
less Mortgage Payoff
= Sale Proceeds Before Taxes

You need to figure out your selling costs. A 5% commission on a $475,000 selling price is $23,750. To that add legal fees of $4,500 for total selling costs of $28,250.

475,000 (Selling Price)
less 28,250 (Costs of Sale)

less 267,000 (Mortgage Payoff)
= 179,750 (Sale Proceeds Before Taxes)

Your total cash flow for Year 7 will be these sale proceeds plus $8,344 cash flow from operations, or $188,094.

After you enter the cash flows, look up the PV factor for each year under the 10.0% discount column. Multiply each cash flow by its corresponding factor to determine its PV, then add up the PVs.

		Factor @ 10.0%	PV
Cash Flow, End of Year 1	3,899	0.909091	3,544.55
Cash Flow, End of Year 2	6,244	0.826446	5,160.33
Cash Flow, End of Year 3	3,111	0.751315	2,337.34
Cash Flow, End of Year 4	4,885	0.683013	3,336.52
Cash Flow, End of Year 5	7,362	0.620921	4,571.22
Cash Flow, End of Year 6	5,905	0.564474	3,333.22
Cash Flow, End of Year 7	188,094	0.513158	96,521.94
Cash Flow, End of Year 8	0	0	0
Cash Flow, End of Year 9	0	0	0
Cash Flow, End of Year 10	0	0	0
TOTAL PV			118,805.12

The Present Value of this series of cash flows to the nearest dollar is $118,805.

17

Net Present Value

I t is a short step from Present Value and Discounted Cash Flow Analysis to Net Present Value (NPV). You'll recall from the previous chapter that DCF gave you the Present Value of the entire future stream of cash flows from your investment. The result was the Present Value of everything coming back to you from your investment in the property. The *Net* Present Value simply takes into account one more cash flow that we didn't talk about in DCF: your initial cash investment.

The NPV is the difference between what you get out of the property, in discounted dollars, and what you put in. When your NPV is positive, it means your rate of return was actually better than the discount rate you chose. When your NPV is negative, it means your true rate of return was less than the discount rate.

Net Present Value (NPV) = Present Value of All Future Cash Flows less Initial Cash Investment

To calculate NPV, you'll begin by doing exactly what you did in Chapter 16; then finish the task by subtracting your initial cash investment.

Problem 17-1:

Revisit problems 16-1 and 16-2. For the property in 16-1, your original cash investment was $105,000. For the property in 16-2, it was $110,000. Calculate the Net Present Value of the income streams described in each problem.

Problem 17-2:

Your purchase a property for $500,00 with a 20% down payment. Its first-year Net Operating Income is $50,000; second-year is $54,000; and third-year is $58,000. Annual debt service is $35,472. You expect to sell the property at the end of the third year, using the same cap rate at which you purchased it to estimate its resale value. You also use that same rate to discount the value of your future cash flows. The selling costs will include 6% brokerage commission and $4,000 legal fees. Your mortgage payoff is $382,223.

What is the Net Present Value of the income stream described here?

Answer 17-1:

For each of these, apply the formula:

Net Present Value (NPV) = Present Value of All Future Cash Flows less Initial Cash Investment

For 16-1, the PV of future cash flows is $110,698 and your initial investment is $105,000.

Net Present Value (NPV) = 110,698 less 105,000

Net Present Value (NPV) = 5,698

For 16-2, the PV of future cash flows is $118,805 and your initial investment is $110,000.

Net Present Value (NPV) = 118,805 less 110,000

Net Present Value (NPV) = 8,805

Answer 17-2:

This problem gives you a chance to practice topics discussed in several of the previous chapters.

In order to calculate the NPV, you need to determine the initial investment and the Present Value of all future cash flows. Start with the initial investment. If the property was purchased for $500,000 with a 20% down payment, then the initial investment – assuming no other costs, since none is mentioned – is $100,000.

Next for the cash flows. You recall this concept from Chapter 13:

    Net Operating Income
    less Debt Service
    = Cash Flow Before Taxes

You can figure the cash flow for each year from the facts given.

Year 1 Cash Flow:

    50,000 (Net Operating Income)
    less 35,472 (Debt Service)
    = 14,528 (Cash Flow Before Taxes)

Year 2 Cash Flow:

    54,000 (Net Operating Income)
    less 35,472 (Debt Service)
    = 18,528 (Cash Flow Before Taxes)

Year 3 Cash Flow:

    58,000 (Net Operating Income)
    less 35,472 (Debt Service)
    = 22,528 (Cash Flow Before Taxes)

To the Year 3 cash flow you must also add the Sale Proceeds, and to do that you'll need to determine the expected selling price. The problem says you will capitalize the NOI using the same rate at which you purchased the property. What was that rate? Return to Chapter 10 for a formula:

Capitalization Rate = Net Operating Income / Value

Since you purchased the property for $500,000 with a NOI of $50,000, the math is easy:

Capitalization Rate = 50,000 / 500,000

Capitalization Rate = 10%

Return to Chapter 10 again for the transposed formula if you need to, so you can now calculate the property's estimated value at the end of Year 3, when it has a NOI of $58,000:

Value = Net Operating Income / Capitalization Rate

Value = 58,000 / 0.10

Value = 580,000

Next you need to determine the Sale Proceeds. The first item to consider is the Costs of Sale. A 6% commission on a $580,000 selling price is $34,800. Add $4,000 in legal fees and you have Costs of Sale totaling $38,800. Now fill in this formula from Chapter 15:

Selling Price
less Costs of Sale
less Mortgage Payoff
= Sale Proceeds Before Taxes

580,000 (Selling Price)
less 38,800 (Costs of Sale)
less 382,223 (Mortgage Payoff)
= 158,977 (Sale Proceeds Before Taxes)

Combine the Sale Proceeds with the $22,528 cash flow from Year 3 for a total Year 3 cash of $181,505.

Finally, you should have enough data to use the Discounted Cash Flow form you saw in Chapter 16:

		Factor @ 10.0%	PV
Cash Flow, End of Year 1	14,528	0.909091	13,207.27
Cash Flow, End of Year 2	18,528	0.826446	15,312.39
Cash Flow, End of Year 3	181,505	0.751315	136,367.43
TOTAL PV			164,887.09

The Present Value of the series of cash flows is $164,887.09. To figure the Net Present Value, subtract the initial investment.

Net Present Value (NPV) = Present Value of All Future Cash Flows less Initial Cash Investment

Net Present Value (NPV) = 164,887 less 100,000

Net Present Value (NPV) = 64,887

18

Profitability Index

T
he Profitability Index is first cousin to Net Present Value. With NPV
you found the difference between the Present Value of all future cash
flows and the initial investment. With Profitability Index, you find the
ratio instead.

**Profitability Index = Present Value of All Future
Cash Flows / Initial Investment**

Is this variation on NPV nothing more than a math exercise? Not really, because the PI allows you to make a meaningful comparison of two properties that
require different amounts of cash up front. The Profitability Index tells you the
proportion of dollars returned to dollars invested, and is not skewed by the
amount of the investment.

Problem 18-1:

You purchase a property with an initial cash investment of $100,000, and project
the following cash flows from operating that property over the next five years:

Cash Flow, End of Year 1	6,000
Cash Flow, End of Year 2	6,750
Cash Flow, End of Year 3	7,300

Cash Flow, End of Year 4	7,900
Cash Flow, End of Year 5	8,800

You expect to sell the property at the end of the fifth year and receive cash proceeds of $140,000. You believe 10% is an appropriate rate at which to discount all of your cash flows. What is your profitability index?

Problem 18-2:

You are comparing two properties as potential investments. Property #1 requires a cash outlay of $100,000. The Present Value of all future cash flows for the next five years, including the resale, is $180,000. Property #2 requires a cash investment of $200,000. The Present Value of its future cash flows, including resale at the end of Year 5, is $320,000. What is the NPV and Profitability Index for each of these properties? Does the property with the greater NPV have the higher Profitability Index?

Answer 18-1:

First you will need to find the Present Value of the future cash flows. You can use the table of 10% PV factors that you had in Chapter 16. Don't forget to add the resale proceeds to your cash for Year 5.

		Factor @ 10.0%	PV
Cash Flow, End of Year 1	6,000	0.909091	5,454.55
Cash Flow, End of Year 2	6,750	0.826446	5,578.51
Cash Flow, End of Year 3	7,300	0.751315	5,484.60
Cash Flow, End of Year 4	7,900	0.683013	5,395.80
Cash Flow, End of Year 5	148,800	0.620921	92,393.04
TOTAL PV			114,306.50

Next apply the formula,

Profitability Index = Present Value of All Future Cash Flows / Initial Investment

Profitability Index = 114,307 / 100,000

Profitability Index = 1.14307

Answer 18-2:

For each property you'll need to apply these two formulas:

Net Present Value (NPV) = Present Value of All Future Cash Flows less Initial Cash Investment

Profitability Index (PI) = Present Value of All Future Cash Flows / Initial Investment

Property #1:

Net Present Value = 180,000 less 100,000

Net Present Value = 80,000

Profitability Index = 180,000 / 100,000

Profitability Index = 1.8

Property #2:

Net Present Value = 320,000 less 200,000

Net Present Value = 120,000

Profitability Index = 320,000 / 200,000

Profitability Index = 1.6

Although Property #2 has a significantly higher NPV, it has a lower Profitability Index. It requires a disproportionately larger initial investment in Property #2 to generate the additional cash. Property #1 has the higher index because it returns more cash per dollar invested.

19

Internal Rate of Return

T
hink back to the discussion of Discounted Cash Flow. You had a series of future cash flows and a given discount rate. You used the rate to discount each of the cash flows back to the present, added up the results, and called that the Present Value of the future cash flows.

Later you took the process one step further with Net Present Value when you subtracted the initial investment from the Present Value of the future cash flows.

What both of these procedures had in common was that you "knew" the discount rate – or at least, you specified the rate to be used, and calculated the Present Value accordingly. With Internal Rate of Return, the discount rate becomes the unknown factor. What discount rate makes the Present Value of the future cash flows equal to what you paid for them, i.e., equal to the initial investment? To put it another way, what discount rate makes the Net Present Value equal to zero? That rate is the Internal Rate of Return.

Put away your pencil. Anyone who thinks it's a good idea to compute IRR manually is so lacking in judgment that they should not be allowed to play with real money. You can compute IRR with Excel, or more simply, you can download an Excel model to do it for you. Go to our site http://www.realdata.com/book.

Problem 19-1:

You purchase a property with a $100,000 cash investment. During the next five years you project the following cash flows:

Cash Flow, End of Year 1	1,000
Cash Flow, End of Year 2	2,000
Cash Flow, End of Year 3	3,000
Cash Flow, End of Year 4	4,000
Cash Flow, End of Year 5	5,000

You expect to sell the property at the End of Year 5 (EOY 5) for $140,000. What is your investment's Internal Rate of Return?

Problem 19-2:

You purchase a property with a $100,000 cash investment. During the next five years you project the following cash flows:

Cash Flow, End of Year 1	8,000
Cash Flow, End of Year 2	5,000
Cash Flow, End of Year 3	4,000
Cash Flow, End of Year 4	3,000
Cash Flow, End of Year 5	2,000

You expect to sell the property at EOY5 for $133,000. What is your investment's Internal Rate of Return?

Problem 19-3:

The total undiscounted cash flow is the same for the properties in problems 19-1 and 19-2, yet one has an IRR that is higher than the other. Why?

Answer 19-1:

Use the IRR Excel model and enter the data. Remember to include the sale proceeds as part of Year 5. Also note that the initial investment is a cash outflow and hence a negative number.

Initial Investment	(100,000)
Cash Flow, End of Year 1	1,000
Cash Flow, End of Year 2	2,000
Cash Flow, End of Year 3	3,000
Cash Flow, End of Year 4	4,000
Cash Flow, End of Year 5	145,000
Internal Rate of Return	9.44%

Answer 19-2:

Again, use the IRR Excel model and enter the data. Remember to include the sale proceeds as part of Year 5.

Initial Investment	(100,000)
Cash Flow, End of Year 1	8,000
Cash Flow, End of Year 2	5,000
Cash Flow, End of Year 3	5,000
Cash Flow, End of Year 4	3,000
Cash Flow, End of Year 5	135,000
Internal Rate of Return	10.07%

Answer 19-3:

Even though the total of the face amount of cash flow is the same for both properties, the time value of money favors the second scenario. In that situation, you receive more cash in the early years, and you recall that money received sooner is more valuable than money received later. Even though the first property delivers $10,000 more upon sale, the fact that you have to wait five years to receive it makes that cash less valuable than the early, larger cash flows in the second example.

Price, Income, and Expenses per Unit

hese measures are unlikely to provide revelatory insights into the worth of an investment property. Nonetheless, they are still used by many brokers and investors, and so you should be familiar with them.

Price per Unit = Price / Number of Rental Units

Income per Unit = Gross Scheduled Income / Number of Rental Units

Expenses per Unit = Operating Expenses / Number of Rental Units

Problem 20-1:

A 50-unit apartment building is offered for sale at $4 million. It has a Gross Scheduled Income of $575,000 and operating expenses of $210,000. What are this property's Price, Income, and Expenses per Unit?

Problem 20-2:

Cedar St. is home to 10 apartment buildings of 50 to 70 units each. Four of the buildings have sold within the last year at an average price of $60,000 per unit. A fifth building, with 60 units has just come on the market. Based on this information, what would you estimate its price to be?

Answer 20-1:

Apply the formulas:

Price per Unit = Price / Number of Rental Units

Price per Unit = 4,000,000 / 50

Price per Unit = 80,000

Income per Unit = Gross Scheduled Income / Number of Rental Units

Income per Unit = 575,000 / 50

Income per Unit = 11,500

Expenses per Unit = Operating Expenses / Number of Rental Units

Expenses per Unit = 210,000 / 50

Expenses per Unit = 4,200

Answer 20-2:

You need to take the formula, Price per Unit = Price / Number of Rental Units, and transpose it to solve for Price:

Price = Number of Rental Units x Price per Unit

Price = 60 x 60,000

Price = 3.6 million

21

Price, Income, and Expenses per Square Foot

I n general, these measures are a bit more useful than those in Chapter 20. That is because most commercial property is leased by the square foot. Keep in mind, however, that local custom will dictate whether the square footage refers to the Gross Building Area or the Net Rentable Area (see Chapter 37). For the purposes of these problems, assume Net Rentable Area.

Price per Square Foot = Price / Gross Building Area or Net Rentable Area

Income per Square Foot = Gross Scheduled Income / Gross Building Area or Net Rentable Area

Expenses per Square Foot = Operating Expenses / Gross Building Area or Net Rentable Area

Problem 21-1:

A building contains 50,000 square feet of Net Rentable Area. Its Gross Scheduled Income is $1 million and its operating expenses equal $150,000. It is offered for sale at $8 million. What are its price, income and expenses per square foot?

Problem 21-2:

A 5,000 square foot retail space rents for $40 per square foot per year. What is the annual rent in total dollars?

Problem 21-3:

Commercial property in a particular Central Business District has been selling for an average of $400 per square foot. You have a 20,000 square foot building in the district. Based on this information, what price might you estimate for your building?

Answer 21-1:

You need to apply these formulas;

Price per Square Foot = Price / Gross Building Area or Net Rentable Area

Price per Square Foot = 8,000,000 / 50,000

Price per Square Foot = 160.00

Income per Square Foot = Gross Scheduled Income / Gross Building Area or Net Rentable Area

Income per Square Foot = 1,000,000 / 50,000

Income per Square Foot = 20.00

Expenses per Square Foot = Operating Expenses / Gross Building Area or Net Rentable Area

Expenses per Square Foot = 150,000 / 50,000

Expenses per Square Foot = 3.00

Answer 21-2:

You need to take the formula, Income per Square Foot = Gross Scheduled Income / Gross Building Area or Net Rentable Area, and transpose it, keeping in mind that the Gross Scheduled Income here applies just to this one unit:

Gross Scheduled Income = Net Rentable Area x Income per Square Foot

Gross Scheduled Income = 5,000 x 40

Gross Scheduled Income = 200,000

Answer 21-3:

You need to transpose the formula, Price per Square Foot = Price / Gross Building Area or Net Rentable Area, to solve for Price:

Price = Price per Square Foot x Gross Building Area or Net Rentable Area

Price = 400 x 20,000

Price = 8,000,000

22

Operating Expense Ratio

I
t can be useful to compare operating expenses among properties in a given market. If a property you're considering reports one or more expenses that seems out of line with similar properties, that information can serve as a red flag, warning you to dig deeper into the source of the information.

For comparison purposes the actual dollar amount of individual expenses may not be as helpful as a proportional measure, such as the ratio of each expense to the Gross Operating Income.

Operating Expense Ratio = Operating Expense / Gross Operating Income

Problem 22-1:

You are considering the purchase of a property whose Gross Operating Income is $40,000. The seller provides the following information about operating expenses:

Advertising	300
Electricity	450
Insurance	2,200

Mortgage Interest	16,500
Real Estate Taxes	4,600
Repairs and Maintenance	3,560
Snow Removal	360
Supplies	275
Trash Removal	1,000
Water	2,200

What is the Operating Expense Ratio for each expense and for the total?

Problem 22-2:

You are looking at a property whose Gross Scheduled Income is $110,000. You expect a 3% loss due to vacancy and credit. Operating expenses are represented as follows:

Accounting	1,200
Advertising	600
Electricity	1,600
Insurance	5,500
Legal	2,000
Property Management	5,000
Real Estate Taxes	11,400
Repairs and Maintenance	7,200
Snow Removal	400
Supplies	700
Trash Removal	1,800
Water	1,600

What is the Operating Expense Ratio for each expense and for the total?

Problem 22-3:

Assume that the properties in the problems above are relatively similar and exist in the same market. Would the comparison of the data for these two properties raise any questions you would want to investigate further?

Answer 22-1:

Before you begin to solve this problem, you need to recognize that something is wrong here – or to paraphrase your friends on Sesame Street – one of these things is not like the others. If you recall the discussion of Net Operating Income in Chapter 9, then you'll also remember that mortgage interest is not an operating expense; so you must remove that from the list.

To calculate the Operating Expense Ratio, you take each expense and divide it by the Gross Operating Income, as per the formula above.

Operating Expense Ratio = Operating Expense / Gross Operating Income

When you do, you come up with the following:

		Operating Expense Ratio
Advertising	300	0.75%
Electricity	450	1.13%
Insurance	2,200	5.50%
Real Estate Taxes	4,600	11.50%
Repairs and Maintenance	3,560	8.90%
Snow Removal	360	0.90%
Supplies	275	0.69%
Trash Removal	1,000	2.50%
Water	2,200	5.50%
TOTAL	14,945	37.36%

Answer 22-2:

You have an additional step here because you need to calculate the Gross Operating Income. To do that, apply the formula from Chapter 8:

Gross Scheduled Income
less Vacancy and Credit Loss
= Gross Operating Income

Fill in your data to obtain the GOI, which is $106,700

110,000 (Gross Scheduled Income)
less 3,300 (Vacancy and Credit Loss, 110,000 x 0.03)
= 106,700 (Gross Operating Income)

Then, as in the previous problem, calculate the Operating Expense Ratio by taking each expense and dividing it by the Gross Operating Income.

		Operating Expense Ratio
Accounting	1,200	1.12%
Advertising	600	0.56%
Electricity	1,600	1.50%
Insurance	5,500	5.15%
Legal	2,000	1.87%
Property Management	5,000	4.69%
Real Estate Taxes	11,400	10.68%
Repairs and Maintenance	7,200	6.75%
Snow Removal	400	0.37%
Supplies	700	0.66%
Trash Removal	1,800	1.69%
Water	1,600	1.50%
TOTAL	39,000	36.55%

Answer 22-3:

Unlike other problems you've worked on so far, this one is not so easily quantifi-
able. Still, you should be able to infer a few possible issues from these numbers.
The second property has two additional expenses, accounting and property management. The smaller property (presumably the one with the lower rent income)
could be self-managed, but wouldn't it be prudent to assume that you would pay
for tax preparation (i.e., accounting) with either one?

Notice also that the cost for Repairs and Maintenance is 8.9% in the first property and 6.75% in the second. Not an enormous difference, but you might want to
investigate the repair costs of some other properties to see which of these is
closer to typical. Perhaps one owner here has a lot that needs fixing, or another
is leaving maintenance problems unaddressed.

Finally, one property is paying 5.5% of its GOI for water, the other 1.5%. There could be a reasonable explanation – perhaps one building has separate water meters for the tenants, plus one for the landlord. Or maybe one has chronically leaky fixtures that are being ignored. The difference in the expense ratios probably warrants further investigation.

23

Debt Coverage Ratio

O ne of the most important metrics you will encounter in your real estate investing is the Debt Coverage Ratio. It is the ratio of Net Operating Income to Debt Service.

Debt Coverage Ratio = Annual Net Operating Income / Annual Debt Service

Why is this important? Virtually every commercial lender applies this measure to assess the level of risk when financing an income property. Remember that the NOI is your income after vacancy and credit loss and after operating expenses, but before debt payments. Hence the DCR tells the lender, proportionally, how much more (or less) money you have than what is absolutely necessary to make your loan payments.

If your NOI and your debt service are exactly the same, the ratio is 1.00. That means you expect to have just enough to make your mortgage payments, without a nickel left over. Your prospective lender will not be happy with that news, and will almost certainly not give you the loan. While the type of property and the location will certainly figure into the underwriting decision, the typical lender will expect you to have a margin of error of 20% or more, which translates into a Debt Coverage Ratio of 1.20 or greater.

Problem 23-1:

Your property has a Net Operating Income of $27,000. You are seeking to re-finance into a loan that will have monthly mortgage payments of $2,000. What is your Debt Coverage Ratio? Do you think your DCR is good enough?

Problem 23-2:

Your property has six units that rent for $1,000 per month each. You allow 3% for vacancy and credit loss and pay the following as operating expenses:

Electricity	550
Insurance	3,700
Miscellaneous	900
Real Estate Taxes	10,800
Repairs and Maintenance	6,700
Water	1,600

You are trying to secure a mortgage that will require a monthly payment of $3,000. What is your Debt Coverage Ratio? Do you think it is good enough?

Problem 23-3:

One of the properties in the problems above had a Debt Coverage Ratio that you suspect will be too low to secure financing. What Net Operating Income would that property need to achieve in order to reach a 1.20 DCR?

Answer 23-1:

Just insert the facts given into the formula:

Debt Coverage Ratio = Annual Net Operating Income / Annual Debt Service

Debt Coverage Ratio = 27,000 / (2,000 x 12)

Debt Coverage Ratio = 27,000 / 24,000

Debt Coverage Ratio = 1.125

Don't hold your breath. With a DCR below 1.20, your chances of getting the loan are slim.

Answer 23-2:

You need to begin by calculating the property's Net Operating Income, as you learned in Chapter 9.

    Gross Scheduled Income
    Less Vacancy and Credit Loss
    = Gross Operating Income
    Less Operating Expenses
    = Net Operating Income

You have six units renting at $1,000 per month. $6,000 per month times 12 months gives you a Gross Scheduled Income of $72,000. You expect to lose 3% of that to vacancy and credit. 3% of $72,000 is $2,160, leaving a Gross Operating Income of $69,840.

Next, add up your operating expenses:

Electricity	550
Insurance	3,700
Miscellaneous	900
Real Estate Taxes	10,800
Repairs and Maintenance	6,700
Water	1,600
TOTAL	24,250

Now you have enough information to fill in the formula for NOI:

72,000 (Gross Scheduled Income)
less 2,160 (Vacancy and Credit Loss)
= 69,840 (Gross Operating Income)

less 24,250 (Operating Expenses)
= 45,590 (Net Operating Income)

At last you can use the formula for Debt Coverage Ratio:

Debt Coverage Ratio = Annual Net Operating Income / Annual Debt Service

Debt Coverage Ratio = 45,590 / (3,000 x 12)

Debt Coverage Ratio = 45,590 / 36,000

Debt Coverage Ratio = 1.27

You know there are no guarantees when chasing financing, but your Debt Coverage Ratio on this deal looks good and should work in your favor.

Answer 23-3:

The property in Problem 23-1 had a DCR of 1.125. In order to find the Net Operating Income necessary to reach 1.20 you'll need to transpose the formula to solve for NOI, treating the DCR as a "given:"

Annual Net Operating Income = Annual Debt Service x Debt Coverage Ratio

Annual Net Operating Income = 24,000 x 1.20

Annual Net Operating Income = 28,800

A NOI of $28,800 will get you to your DCR threshold of 1.20.

24

Break-Even Ratio

T he Break-Even Ratio (BER), also called the Default Ratio, is one of several underwriting measures used by lenders. (See also the Debt Coverage Ratio, Chapter 23, and the Loan-to-Value Ratio, Chapter 26.)

The Break-Even Ratio expresses the relationship between your property's outgo and its income. Lenders generally look for a BER of 85% or less.

Break-Even Ratio = (Debt Service + Operating Expenses) / Gross Operating Income

Problem 24-1:

You have a property with a Gross Operating Income of $50,000 and operating expenses of $21,500. Your monthly mortgage payment is $1,744. What is the property's Break-Even Ratio?

Problem 24-2:

You have a 9,000 square foot commercial property that rents, on average, for $22 per square foot. You allow for vacancy and credit loss of 3%. Operating expenses total $47,500. Your monthly mortgage payment is $8,922. What is the property's Break-Even Ratio?

Problem 24-3:

You have a property with annual operating expenses of $18,000 and a monthly mortgage payment of $1,551. What Gross Operating Income would you need if your lender's required Break-Even Ratio is 85%?

Problem 24-4:

You want to refinance a small office building that has a Gross Operating Income of $120,000 and operating expenses of $37,000. Your lender requires a Break-Even Ratio of 80% or less. Given just these facts, what is the greatest monthly mortgage payment that your lender might approve?

Answer 24-1:

Apply the formula,

Break-Even Ratio = (Debt Service + Operating Expenses) / Gross Operating Income

Break-Even Ratio = (1,744 x 12 + 21,500) / 50,000

Break-Even Ratio = (20,928 + 21,500) / 50,000

Break-Even Ratio = (42,428) / 50,000

Break-Even Ratio = 84.9%

Answer 24-2:

First you need to calculate the Gross Operating Income using the formula from Chapter 8:

Gross Scheduled Income
less Vacancy and Credit Loss
= Gross Operating Income

Fill in the data to find that your GOI is $192,060.

198,000 (Gross Scheduled Income, 9,000 sf x 22 per sf)
less 5,940 (Vacancy and Credit Loss, 198,000 x 0.03)
= 192,060 (Gross Operating Income)

Now use the formula for Break-Even Ratio:

Break-Even Ratio = (Debt Service + Operating Expenses) / Gross Operating Income

Break-Even Ratio = (8,922 x 12 + 47,500) / 192,060

Break-Even Ratio = (107,064 + 47,500) / 192,060

Break-Even Ratio = (154,564) / 192,060

Break-Even Ratio = 80.5%

Answer 24-3:

Back to Algebra I again. You need to transpose the Break-Even Ratio formula to solve for the Gross Operating Income.

Gross Operating Income = (Debt Service + Operating Expenses) / Break-Even Ratio

Gross Operating Income = (1,551 x 12 + 18,000) / 0.85

Gross Operating Income = (18,612 + 18,000) / 0.85

Gross Operating Income = (36,612) / 0.85

Gross Operating Income = 43,073 (to the nearest dollar)

Answer 24-4:

Another formula transposition is needed, this time to solve for the annual debt service. You can do pretty much anything to an equation, provided you do the *same* thing to both sides. Your objective is to get the debt service alone on one side of the equal sign. Take the BER equation,

Break-Even Ratio = (Debt Service + Operating Expenses) / Gross Operating Income

and multiply both sides by the Gross Operating Income. That will give you the following:

(Break-Even Ratio x Gross Operating Income) = (Debt Service + Operating Expenses)

Then subtract operating expenses from both sides.

(Break-Even Ratio x Gross Operating Income) – Operating Expenses = Debt Service

Since you've been accustomed to seeing the unknown on the left, you can flip the formula around.

Debt Service = (Break-Even Ratio x Gross Operating Income) – Operating Expenses

From here, things are pretty straightforward.

Debt Service = (0.80 x 120,000) – 37,000

Debt Service = 96,000 – 37,000

Debt Service = 59,000

One final wrinkle. The problem asked you to compute the maximum monthly mortgage payment, but you just solved for the annual debt service so you need to divide this by 12 to find that the maximum monthly payment would be $4,916.67.

59,000 / 12 = 4,916.67

25

Return on Equity

Although Return on Equity is a measure more common to business analysis, in *What Every Real Estate Investor Needs to Know About Cash Flow...* I discuss two approaches to ROE as that measure applies to real estate. One is the typical relationship between Cash Flow After Taxes and Initial Investment:

Return on Equity = Cash Flow After Taxes / Initial Investment

The second method looks at the equity component not as your initial investment, but rather as your current "unrealized" equity, i.e., the difference between the property's value and its outstanding debt. A property's value may grow and its debt decline over time so that this unrealized equity becomes greater than the initial investment. You can express ROE using this unrealized equity as follows:

Return on Equity = Cash Flow After Taxes / (Resale Value less Mortgage Balance)

This latter approach may help you discern when your equity is growing disproportionately to the cash flow it generates. Your Return on Equity could drop not because your cash flow is weak but rather because your equity has become so great; and that should prompt you to ask if you should extract some or all of that equity to invest elsewhere.

Problem 25-1:

You have a property with a Cash Flow After Taxes of $5,000. You purchased it with an initial cash investment of $60,000. The current mortgage balance is $235,000 and the property's resale value is $300,000. Calculate the Return on Equity using each of the methods described above.

Problem 25-2:

You purchase a property for $1 million with a $700,000 first mortgage. The first-year Cash Flow After Taxes is $17,200, and the Net Operating Income is $121,000. The market capitalization rate is 11%. At the end of the first year your mortgage balance is $685,000. Calculate the Return on Equity using each of the methods above.

Answer 25-1:

Use the formula for the first method:

Return on Equity = Cash Flow After Taxes / Initial Investment

Return on Equity = 5,000 / 60,000

Return on Equity = 8.33%

The second method:

Return on Equity = Cash Flow After Taxes / (Resale Value less Mortgage Balance)

Return on Equity = 5,000 / (300,000 less 235,000)

Return on Equity = 5,000 / 65,000

Return on Equity = 7.69%

Answer 25-2:

From the facts given you need to calculate the amount of your initial investment. You purchased the property for $1 million with a $700,000 first mortgage, so you invested $300,000.

You also need to estimate the current resale value using one of the capitalization formulas from Chapter 10:

Value = Net Operating Income / Capitalization Rate

Value = 121,000 / 0.11

Value = 1,100,000

Now you can apply each of the ROE formulas.

Return on Equity = Cash Flow After Taxes / Initial Investment

Return on Equity = 17,200 / 300,000

Return on Equity = 5.73%

Also,

Return on Equity = Cash Flow After Taxes / (Resale Value less Mortgage Balance)

Return on Equity = 17,200 / (1,100,000 less 685,000)

Return on Equity = 17,200 / (415,000)

Return on Equity = 4.14%

26

Loan-to-Value Ratio

The Loan-to-Value Ratio (LTV) is another measurement used by lenders when underwriting mortgage loans. (See also Chapter 23, Debt Coverage Ratio and Chapter 24, Break-Even Ratio) Although the name would appear to say it all, "Value" has a very specific meaning when used with this measurement. It is the *lesser* of the property's appraised value or its actual sale price. If a property appraises at a value that is higher than your purchase price, don't expect your lender to give you X% of that higher valuation.

Loan-to-Value Ratio = Loan Amount / Lesser of Property's Appraised Amount or Actual Selling Price

If you have or are seeking more than one mortgage against a property (for example, applying for a second mortgage, or for a new first while subordinating an existing second), the lender will almost certainly treat the total of all loans as the "Loan Amount" for LTV purposes. In other words, even if you are applying for a particular loan that, by itself, is under the lender's LTV threshold, you usually need to keep the total of all loans under that threshold in order to qualify.

Problem 26-1:

You are purchasing a property for $1 million. The lender's appraisal is $1.05 million. You are applying for a loan of $780,000. What Loan-to-Value Ratio does your loan request represent?

Problem 26-2:

Your lender's maximum Loan-to-Value Ratio is 80%. You are purchasing a property for $520,000. The lender's appraisal estimates its value at $500,000. Given just these facts, what is the largest loan you can expect against this property?

Problem 26-3:

The appraiser in Problem 26-2 discovers that he pressed the wrong key on his Smith-Corona typewriter when preparing the appraisal report. The bottom line should have been a valuation of $550,000, not $500,000. Might this change the amount the lender is willing to give? If so, then what is the correct amount?

Problem 26-4:

You own a property whose current mortgage balance is $400,000. You want to get a second mortgage in order to make improvements and additions to the property. The lender's appraisal is $700,000. If your secondary lender's maximum LTV ratio is 75%, what is the maximum new money you can expect to borrow?

Answer 26-1:

First you need to take note of which is less, the selling price or the appraised value. In this problem it is the selling price of $1 million. Next you apply the LTV formula.

Loan-to-Value Ratio = Loan Amount / Lesser of Property's Appraised Amount or Actual Selling Price

Loan-to-Value Ratio = 780,000 / 1,000,000

Loan-to-Value Ratio = 78%

Answer 26-2:

Again you need to begin by observing which is less, the selling price or the appraised value. In this problem it is the appraised value of $500,000. Next you must transpose the LTV formula to solve for the loan amount.

Loan-to-Value Ratio = Loan Amount / Lesser of Property's Appraised Amount or Actual Selling Price

Loan Amount = Lesser of Property's Appraised Amount or Actual Selling Price x Loan-to-Value Ratio

Finally, you enter the data and solve for the loan amount of $400,000"

Loan Amount = 500,000 x 0.80

Loan Amount = 400,000

Answer 26-3:

Now that the appraisal has been changed to $550,000, it is the selling price of $520,000 that is the lesser amount.

As before, you need to use the transposed form of the LTV formula to solve for the loan amount.

Loan Amount = Lesser of Property's Appraised Amount or Actual Selling Price x Loan-to-Value Ratio

You enter the revised data and solve for the loan amount of $416,000.

Loan Amount = 520,000 x 0.80

Loan Amount = 416,000

Answer 26-4:

In this problem there is no sale transaction; you already own the property. Since there is no sale, the "Value" must be the appraised value.

Once again you need to use the transposed formula so you can solve for the loan amount. Keep in mind, however, that you'll be solving for the maximum combined first and second mortgages.

Loan Amount = Lesser of Property's Appraised Amount or Actual Selling Price x Loan-to-Value Ratio

Loan Amount = 700,000 x .75

Loan Amount = 525,000

$525,000 is the highest total indebtedness this lender will accept. You already have a first mortgage of $400,000, so the difference of $125,000 is the maximum second mortgage amount that you can expect this lender to approve.

525,000 less 400,000 = 125,000 maximum second mortgage

27

Points

"Points" refer specifically to loan points, a premium you pay to a lender for making a loan. A point equals one percent of the loan amount.

One Point = Dollar Amount of Loan / 100

Often more useful is this variation:

Dollar Amount of Points Paid = Mortgage Loan Amount x No. of Points / 100

Problem 27-1:

You apply for a $300,000 loan that requires you to pay 1.5 points. What is the cost of the points?

Problem 27-2:

You apply for $450,000 20-year loan at 7.375% with 1.625 points. What is the cost of the points?

Answer 27-1:

You will use the second formula, above, to find that you will pay $4,500 in points.

Dollar Amount of Points Paid = Mortgage Loan Amount x No. of Points / 100

Dollar Amount of Points Paid = 300,000 x 1.5 / 100

Dollar Amount of Points Paid = 4,500

Answer 27-2:

Again use the second formula, above, to find that you will pay $7,312.50 in points. Note that the interest rate and the term of the loan have no significance in calculating the points you must pay.

Dollar Amount of Points Paid = Mortgage Loan Amount x No. of Points / 100

Dollar Amount of Points Paid = 450,000 x 1.625 / 100

Dollar Amount of Points Paid = 7,312.50

28

Mortgage Payment / Mortgage Constant

A lthough there are many ways of structuring a mortgage, the most common is as a loan that amortizes over time with fixed periodic payments (usually monthly) of both interest and principal. This chapter shows you how to calculate that periodic payment.

There are several ways you can arrive at a mortgage payment amount.

1. You have probably seen bankers or real estate agents use a book that allows them to look up the payment on a principal amount to the nearest $1,000 at a given rate and term.

2. At the other end of the degree-of-difficulty scale, is the formula,

$$\text{Payment} = PV \frac{i\,(1+i)^{n}}{(1+i)^{n}-1}$$

where PV is the amount of the loan, i is the periodic interest rate and n is the number of periods. Unless you have a degree in math, you may find this approach unappealing.

3. You can download a table called, "Monthly Mortgage Payment per $1" at http://www.realdata.com/book. Below is a small section of that table. Technically speaking, this is a table of mortgage constants. A mortgage constant is the periodic payment amount on a loan of $1 at a particular interest rate and term. If you know the constant for a loan of $1, you can multiply it by the actual number of dollars of the loan to find the payment.

Payment = Loan Amount x Mortgage Constant

Monthly Mortgage Payment per $1 – Mortgage Constant

Years	7.000%	7.125%	7.250%	7.375%	7.500%	7.625%
20	0.00775299	0.00782820	0.00790376	0.00797967	0.00805593	0.00813254
21	0.00758472	0.00766091	0.00773747	0.00781439	0.00789166	0.00796929
22	0.00743424	0.00751140	0.00758893	0.00766684	0.00774510	0.00782374
23	0.00729919	0.00737730	0.00745579	0.00753465	0.00761389	0.00769350
24	0.00717760	0.00725663	0.00733605	0.00741586	0.00749605	0.00757662
25	0.00706779	0.00714773	0.00722807	0.00730880	0.00738991	0.00747141
26	0.00696838	0.00704920	0.00713043	0.00721206	0.00729407	0.00737648
27	0.00687815	0.00695984	0.00704194	0.00712444	0.00720734	0.00729063
28	0.00679609	0.00687862	0.00696157	0.00704492	0.00712868	0.00721282
29	0.00672130	0.00680466	0.00688843	0.00697262	0.00705720	0.00714218
30	0.00665302	0.00673719	0.00682176	0.00690675	0.00699215	0.00707794

4. Yet another way to find the periodic payment is to use Microsoft Excel. The Excel PMT function looks like this:

=PMT(Periodic Rate, Number of Periods, -Present Value)

You can enter this formula into a cell on an Excel worksheet, substituting values for the variables. Note that you should enter the PV (the amount of the loan) as a negative number.

If you don't feel like typing in the formula, you can download a pre-made Excel spreadsheet from http://www.realdata.com/book that will allow you to enter the variables on the worksheet and display the result.

N	%i	Pmt	PV	
0	0.00%	n/a	0.00	calculate payment

Enter the number of periods (i.e., number of payments) under "N;" the interest rate per period under "%i;" and the amount of the loan under "PV."

Problem 28-1:

Use methods 3, 4 and 5 above to calculate the monthly payment on a $450,000 loan at 7.375% for 25 years.

Problem 28-2:

What would the payment be if your rate on the loan in Problem 28-1 were ¼% less? If it were ¼% more? Again, use all three methods.

Answer 28-1:

First solve the problem with the table of mortgage constants. You find the intersection of 7.375% and 25 years to determine that the constant is 0.00730880. Then you multiply the amount of the mortgage by that constant.

Payment = Loan Amount x Mortgage Constant

Payment = 450,000 x 0.00730880

Payment = 3,288.96

Next, use Microsoft Excel's PMT formula. Note that you need to convert the annual interest rate to a monthly rate, and the term of the loan from years to months because you want the payment to be computed as the monthly amount.

=PMT(Periodic Rate, Number of Periods, -Present Value)

=PMT(0.07375/12, 25*12, -450,000)

If you enter the periodic rate and the term as shown in the row above, Excel will calculate them internally; or you can type them in directly yourself:

=PMT(0.006145833, 300, -450,000)

Excel displays the result in the cell, $3,288.96

Finally enter the same variables into the pre-made Excel template. You can enter =0.07375 / 12 for the periodic rate. The model displays only a few decimal places of the periodic interest rate, but it calculates using a longer, more precise rate.

N	%i	Pmt	PV	
300	0.61%	**3,288.96**	450,000.00	calculate payment

Answer 28-2:

This problem was designed to ferret out the fractionally challenged. Can you take $7^3/_8$ and add or subtract $1/_4$? Your ambition to become chairman of the Federal Reserve may depend on it.

$7^3/_8$ plus $1/_4$ is $7^5/_8$, aka 7.625. $7^3/_8$ minus $1/_4$ will give you $7^1/_8$, or 7.125. Now you can use methods 3, 4, and 5 with each of these rates.

For the mortgage constant approach the constant for 7.125% over 25 years is 0.00714773, and for 7.625% it is 0.00747141.

Payment = Loan Amount x Mortgage Constant

Payment = 450,000 x 0.00714773

Payment = 3,216.48 at 7.125%

Payment = 450,000 x 0.00747141

Payment = 3,362.13 at 7.625%

Next, with Microsoft Excel's PMT formula, first at 7.125%:

=PMT(Periodic Rate, Number of Periods, -Present Value)

=PMT(0.07125/12, 25*12, -450,000)

=PMT(0.00593750, 300, -450,000)

Excel displays the result in the cell, $3,216.48

Next at 7.625%:

=PMT(Periodic Rate, Number of Periods, -Present Value)

=PMT(0.07625/12, 25*12, -450,000)

=PMT(0.006354167, 300, -450,000)

Excel displays the result in the cell, $3,362.13

Finally, the pre-made Excel template, first at 7.125%, then at 7.625%:

N	%i	Pmt	PV	
300	0.59%	**3,216.48**	450,000.00	calculate payment

N	%i	Pmt	PV	
300	0.64%	**3,362.13**	450,000.00	calculate payment

29

Principal Balance / Balloon Payment

W ith any amortizing mortgage, you'll find that the principal declines with each payment. You may need to know the loan balance at a particular point in time because you are selling or refinancing, or because you have an obligation to pay off the balance before the loan is fully retired (called a "balloon" payment).

As with the payment calculation in the previous chapter, there are a number of ways you can go about finding the principal balance.

1. Just for the record, you can do it the hard way:

   $$PV = A \times (1 + i)^n - (pmt / i) \times [(1 + i)^n - 1])$$

   Where PV = the Present Value (balance) of the loan, A = the original balance, n is the number of payments made and i is the periodic rate.

2. Somewhat simpler is to use the table of mortgage constants ("Monthly Mortgage Payment per $1"), also discussed in the previous chapter. Use this formula:

   PV = Loan Payment / Mortgage Constant for the rate and remaining term of the loan

Keep in mind that if you are using a monthly payment, then you must also use a monthly mortgage constant.

3. Those readers who have traded in their No. 3 pencil for a computer can use Microsoft Excel. Type this formula into a worksheet cell, replacing the variables with the terms relevant to your loan:

=PV(Periodic Rate, Number of Periods, -Periodic Payment)

It is essential to note that the Number of Periods is the number of payments *remaining* on the loan, and that the Periodic Payment amount must be entered as a negative number.

4. You can use the same pre-made Excel template that you saw in the previous chapter. This time, use the second row to calculate the PV. N is the number of payments remaining.

N	%i	Pmt	PV	
0	0.00%	n/a	0.00	calculate payment
0	0.00%	0.00	**0.00**	calculate present value

5. Perhaps the most useful approach to the issue of loan balance is a loan amortization schedule. This is a table that steps through the entire progress of a loan, showing the principal and interest component of each payment, and the balance remaining after the payment is made. You could build one with Excel, but you don't have to because we provide one you can download at http://www.realdata.com/book.

Problem 29-1:

You have a mortgage whose original balance was $200,000. The interest rate is 7% and the original term was 25 years. Your monthly payment has been $1,413.56. Thirty-six months have elapsed, during which you have made all of your payments on time. Use methods 2, 3 and 4 above to calculate the outstanding loan balance.

Problem 29-2:

You have a mortgage whose original balance was $475,000. The interest rate is 7.625% and the original term was 15 years. Forty-seven months have elapsed, during which you have made all of your $4,437.12 monthly payments on time. Use methods 3 and 4 above to calculate the outstanding loan balance.

Problem 29-3:

Now use the amortization schedule described in method #5 above. For each of the loans in Problems 29-1 and 29-2, what is the balance at the end of month 47? You're going to sell both properties exactly half way between the end of month 47 and the end of 48. How much will the bank require as payoffs on these loans?

Answer 29-1:

First you're going to solve the problem with the table of mortgage constants and with this formula:

PV = Loan Payment / Mortgage Constant for the rate and remaining term of the loan

You can thumb back just a few pages to the table of mortgage constants. Because 36 months have elapsed on your 25-year loan, you're looking for the constant that corresponds to 22 years at 7%.

PV = 1,413.56 / 0.00743424

PV = 190,141.83

Next you'll try this using Excel's PV function.

=PV(Periodic Rate, Number of Periods, – Periodic Payment)

=PV(0.07/12, 300-36, -1413.56)

Note that you can do some of your interim math right inside the Excel function. In this case you are able to divide 7% by 12 to get the monthly rate, and subtract 36 from 300 to find the number of months remaining on the loan.

Excel displays the result, 190,141.80.

Whoops. Not that it's a big deal, but this result is $0.03 less than what you got with the table of constants. There must be a small amount of rounding error creeping into one of these calculations. Perhaps the pre-made template in method #4 will be the tie-breaker.

Again, you can do your interim math right inside each cell. To find the period rate, enter =.07/12 under %i. Speaking of rounding, the number displayed will be rounded, but the underlying value will not. Do the same for N, entering =300-36. You'll get this result:

N	%i	Pmt	PV	
0	0.00%	n/a	0.00	calculate payment
264	0.58%	1,413.56	**190,141.80**	calculate present value

$190,141.80 appears to be the consensus. The table of factors can display only a limited number of decimal places, so it's not unreasonable that a slight rounding error could intrude.

Answer 29-2:

For this problem, you'll forego the table and use just the Excel function and the template. First the function:

=PV(Periodic Rate, Number of Periods, – Periodic Payment)

=PV(0.07625/12, 180-47, -4437.12)

Excel displays the result, 397,568.85

Next you'll use the template. Enter N, %i, and PMT; the result again is 397,568.85.

N	%i	Pmt	PV	
0	0.00%	n/a	0.00	calculate payment
133	0.64%	4,437.12	**397,568.85**	calculate present value

Answer 29-3:

You can download a simple Excel-based amortization schedule at http://www.realdata.com/book. If, in real life, you find yourself contending with more complex loan structures, such as varying payment or compounding frequencies, interest-only switching to amortized, variable rates, fixed principal, skipped payments, etc., you'll find solutions at our main site, http://www.realdata.com.

First, enter the data from the loan in Problem 29-1:

Beginning Balance:	200,000.00		Ann. Int. Rate:	7.000 %
Term, Months:	300		First Pmt Month:	1
Calculated Pmt:	$1,413.56		First Pmt Year:	2011

You're interested in seeing how this loan looks near the end of the fourth year, so skip down a few pages:

	INTEREST	PRINCIPAL	BALANCE
January	1,109.16	304.40	189,837.13
February	1,107.38	306.18	189,530.95
March	1,105.60	307.96	189,222.99
April	1,103.80	309.76	188,913.23
May	1,101.99	311.57	188,601.66
June	1,100.18	313.38	188,288.28
July	1,098.35	315.21	187,973.07
August	1,096.51	317.05	187,656.02
September	1,094.66	318.90	187,337.12
October	1,092.80	320.76	187,016.36
November	1,090.93	322.63	186,693.73
December	1,089.05	324.51	186,369.22
Total 2014	**13,190.41**	**3,772.31**	

Month 47 will be November of the fourth year, so your balance will be $186,693.73. Keep in mind that rounding unavoidably occurs in a table like this, so don't be surprised to see a very small difference between the amortization schedule and the calculation performed with a Present Value function.

One question remains. If you pay this loan off in the middle of the 48th month, December, how much will the bank expect to receive? They will want the outstanding balance as of your last payment – $186,693.73 – but they'll also want interest on that amount until the payoff date. A full month's interest for December would be $1,089.05, so half of that, $544.53, is needed to cover the interest until your December 15 payoff. Hence the total due is

186,693.73 + 544.53, or $187,238.26.

You'll re-work the loan from Problem 29-2 in exactly the same way:

Beginning Balance:	475,000.00	Ann. Int. Rate:	7.625 %
Term, Months:	180	First Pmt Month:	1
Calculated Pmt:	$4,437.12	First Pmt Year:	2011

Scrolling down to the fourth year, you find the outstanding balance at the end of month 47 (November) is $397,568.40.

	INTEREST	PRINCIPAL	BALANCE
January	2,654.83	1,782.29	416,026.26
February	2,643.50	1,793.62	414,232.64
March	2,632.10	1,805.02	412,427.62
April	2,620.63	1,816.49	410,611.13
May	2,609.09	1,828.03	408,783.10
June	2,597.48	1,839.64	406,943.46
July	2,585.79	1,851.33	405,092.13
August	2,574.02	1,863.10	403,229.03
September	2,562.18	1,874.94	401,354.09
October	2,550.27	1,886.85	399,467.24
November	2,538.28	1,898.84	397,568.40
December	2,526.22	1,910.90	395,657.50
Total 2014	**31,094.39**	**22,151.05**	

A payoff on December 15 would require half of the $2,526.22 interest for that month, bringing the total payoff to $398,831.51.

30

Principal and Interest per Period

The amortization schedule of the previous chapter makes it clear that each successive loan payment allocates a little less to interest and a little more to principal. This process of allocation is exactly what the amortization schedule is doing, one payment at a time.

Interest Portion = Outstanding Principal Balance x Periodic Rate

Principal Portion = Payment Amount less Interest Portion

Problem 30-1:

You take out a $300,000 loan at 6% for 30 years. How much of the first payment goes to interest and how much to principal?

Problem 30-2:

For the loan in the previous problem, how much will go to interest and principal for the second and third payments? Find the answers first using the formulas, then confirm them with an amortization schedule.

Answer 30-1:

You begin by determining the monthly payment amount for this loan. Use the Excel PMT function from Chapter 28:

=PMT(Periodic Rate, Number of Periods, -Present Value)

=PMT(.06/12, 360, -300000)

Excel displays the payment amount, 1,798.65.

Confirm this with the pre-made template.

N	%i	Pmt	PV	
360	0.50%	**1,798.65**	300,000.00	calculate payment

Now calculate the interest portion of the first payment.

Interest Portion = Outstanding Principal Balance x Periodic Rate

Interest Portion = 300,000 x 0.005

Interest Portion = 1,500

The portion of the payment that is not interest must be principal.

Principal Portion = Payment Amount less Interest Portion

Principal Portion = 1,798.65 less 1,500.00

Principal Portion = 298.65

Answer 30-2:

To find the interest component of the second payment, you need to calculate the balance that is outstanding after the first payment.

The loan began as $300,000 and you paid $298.65 in principal with your first payment. The difference, $299,701.35 is the amount now outstanding.

Interest Portion = Outstanding Principal Balance x Periodic Rate

Interest Portion = 299,701.35 x 0.005

Interest Portion = 1,498.51 (rounded)

Calculate the principal portion of the payment.

Principal Portion = Payment Amount less Interest Portion

Principal Portion = 1,798.65 less 1,498.51

Principal Portion = 300.14

You have further reduced the balance by $300.14, so after the second payment you owe $299,701.35 less $300.14, or $299,401.21.

Continue now with the third payment.

Interest Portion = Outstanding Principal Balance x Periodic Rate

Interest Portion = 299,401.21 x 0.005

Interest Portion = 1,497.01 (rounded)

Calculate the principal portion of the payment.

Principal Portion = Payment Amount less Interest Portion

Principal Portion = 1,798.65 less 1,497.01

Principal Portion = 301.64

Your balance is now $299,401.21 less $301.64, or $299,099.57.

Finally, confirm your calculation with an amortization schedule:

Beginning Balance:	300,000.00	Ann. Int. Rate:	6.000 %
Term, Months:	360	First Pmt Month:	1
Calculated Pmt:	$1,798.65	First Pmt Year:	2011

	INTEREST	PRINCIPAL	BALANCE
January	1,500.00	298.65	299,701.35
February	1,498.51	300.14	299,401.21
March	1,497.01	301.64	299,099.57

31

Maximum Loan Amount

L enders who underwrite loans on income-producing investment property are always concerned with the property's ability to generate sufficient income to cover the debt comfortably. Before you apply for a loan, you may want to know just how warm or chilly a reception you're likely to receive when you present your application.

To that end it can be helpful to estimate the maximum loan that seems reasonable, given your property's Net Operating Income, the lender's minimum Debt Coverage Ratio, and the loan terms that are available from that lender. With this information and a handy formula you can back your way into the maximum loan amount that is likely to fly.

Maximum Loan Amount = Net Operating Income / Minimum Debt Coverage Ratio / (Monthly Mortgage Constant x 12)

Problem 31-1:

You own a property with a Net Operating Income of $110,000. You would like to refinance this property with a lender who is offering commercial mortgages at 7.125% for 20 years. The lender requires a Debt Coverage Ratio no less than 1.25. Given just this information, what is the largest loan the lender is likely to approve on your property?

Problem 31-2:

You are considering the purchase of a property for $580,000. It appraises for exactly that amount. It has a Gross Scheduled Income of $80,000 and operating expenses of $32,000. You allow 3% for vacancy and credit loss. The most favorable terms you can find are 7% for 25 years from a lender that requires a Debt Coverage Ratio of 1.30 and a Loan-to-Value Ratio no greater than 70%. What is the largest loan you can expect from this lender?

Answer 31-1:

You'll need the formula shown above.

Maximum Loan Amount = Net Operating Income / Minimum Debt Coverage Ratio / (Monthly Mortgage Constant x 12)

You'll also need the table of mortgage constants that you have used for earlier problems.

Monthly Mortgage Payment per $1 – Mortgage Constant

Years	7.000%	7.125%	7.250%	7.375%	7.500%	7.625%
20	0.00775299	0.00782820	0.00790376	0.00797967	0.00805593	0.00813254
21	0.00758472	0.00766091	0.00773747	0.00781439	0.00789166	0.00796929
22	0.00743424	0.00751140	0.00758893	0.00766684	0.00774510	0.00782374
23	0.00729919	0.00737730	0.00745579	0.00753465	0.00761389	0.00769350
24	0.00717760	0.00725663	0.00733605	0.00741586	0.00749605	0.00757662
25	0.00706779	0.00714773	0.00722807	0.00730880	0.00738991	0.00747141
26	0.00696838	0.00704920	0.00713043	0.00721206	0.00729407	0.00737648
27	0.00687815	0.00695984	0.00704194	0.00712444	0.00720734	0.00729063
28	0.00679609	0.00687862	0.00696157	0.00704492	0.00712868	0.00721282
29	0.00672130	0.00680466	0.00688843	0.00697262	0.00705720	0.00714218
30	0.00665302	0.00673719	0.00682176	0.00690675	0.00699215	0.00707794

Maximum Loan Amount = 110,000 / 1.25 / (0.00782820 x 12)

Maximum Loan Amount = 110,000 / 1.25 / (0.0939384)

Notice that you have daisy-chained division. Take it one step at a time.

Maximum Loan Amount = 88,000 / (0.0939384)

Maximum Loan Amount = 936,784

Answer 31-2:

You need to start by calculating the Net Operating Income as you learned in Chapter 9.

Gross Scheduled Income
less Vacancy and Credit Loss
= Gross Operating Income
less Operating Expenses
= Net Operating Income

Fill in the facts:

80,000 (Gross Scheduled Income)
less 2,400 (Vacancy and Credit Loss, 3% of 80,000)
= 77,600 (Gross Operating Income)
less 32,000 (Operating Expenses)
= 45,600 (Net Operating Income)

Next, look up the mortgage constant for a 25-year loan at 7%. You should find that it is 0.00706779.

Now use the maximum loan formula.

Maximum Loan Amount = Net Operating Income / Minimum Debt Coverage Ratio / (Monthly Mortgage Constant x 12)

Maximum Loan Amount = 45,600 / 1.30 / (0.00706779 x 12)

Maximum Loan Amount = 45,600 / 1.30 / (0.08481348)

Maximum Loan Amount = 35,076.92 / (0.08481348)

Maximum Loan Amount = 413,577

Based on the property's income, you should be able to secure a loan of about $413,500.

However, remember that your lender also has a Loan-to-Value constraint. If necessary, do a hasty retreat to Chapter 26 to review this formula:

Loan Amount = Lesser of Property's Appraised Amount or Actual Selling Price x Loan-to-Value Ratio

You are purchasing this property for its appraised value of $580,000 and your lender will accept a LTV no greater than 70%.

Loan Amount = 580,000 x 0.70

Loan Amount = 406,000

Although this property's income should support a loan of $413,500, the lender's Loan-to-Value requirement will limit you a bit further, capping the loan at $406,000.

32

Assessed Value, Property Taxes, and Value Indicated by Assessment

I n most areas of the U.S., real property is taxed first by being appraised. Then an "assessment ratio" is applied to that appraised value to yield an "assessed value," i.e. a value for tax purposes. Finally, a tax rate is applied to the assessed value to determine the property tax owed.

There are perhaps two situations where this mathematical St. Vitus dance may interest you. The first is when your local tax district is discussing a new tax rate. You'll want to see how that will affect your tax bill, and you'll do so with this simple formula:

Property Taxes = Assessed Value x Tax Rate

The second situation is when you might want to back into the district's appraised value of your property, based on its assessed value and the assessment ratio.

Appraised Value = Assessed Value / Assessment Ratio

Problem 32-1:

Your home has an assessed value of $278,000. The tax rate last year was $32 per $1,000 of assessed value. The Town Council is discussing raising the rate to $35. What was you tax bill last year, and what will it be if the Council has its way?

Problem 32-2:

Your town assigns an assessed value, for tax purposes, equal to 70% of the appraised value. What does the Town think your home, as described in Problem 32-1, is worth?

Answer 32-1:

Use the property tax formula shown above:

Property Taxes = Assessed Value x Tax Rate

Since your tax rate was $32 per $1,000 last year you can express it as 0.032.

Property Taxes = 278,000 x 0.032

Property Taxes (last year) = 8,896

This year's proposed tax rate is 35 / 1000 or 0.035.

Property Taxes = 278,000 x 0.035

Property Taxes (this year) = 9,730

Answer 32-2:

To back into the appraised value from the assessment data, use the second formula shown above.

Appraised Value = Assessed Value / Assessment Ratio

Appraised Value = 278,000 / 0.70

Appraised Value = 397,143

33

Adjusted Basis

I n order to calculate the profit, or "gain," when you sell a property (see Chapter 35) you need to know its selling price and its Adjusted Basis. The gain is the difference between the two. Under the tax rules at this writing, the Adjusted Basis is calculated as follows:

Original basis (purchase price and closing costs)
plus Capital Additions
plus Costs of Sale
less Cumulative Depreciation, Real Estate
less Cumulative Depreciation, Capital Additions
= Adjusted Basis

Note that Capital Additions and Capital Improvements are synonymous for our purposes.

Problem 33-1:

You purchase a property for $500,000. During your ownership you make $50,000 in capital improvements. You sell the property after accumulating $30,000 in depreciation on the real estate and $3,000 on the improvements. Your Costs of Sale are $38,500. What is your Adjusted Basis?

Problem 33-2:

You purchase a property for $800,000. In the first year you make a capital addition of $40,000. In the third year you make another, costing $30,000. When you sell the property, you have accumulated $5,100 in depreciation on the first addition and $1,500 on the second. You have also accumulated $76,000 in depreciation on the original property. Your Costs of Sale are 7% of the selling price, which is $900,000. What is your Adjusted Basis?

Answer 33-1:

Take the formula shown at the beginning of the chapter.

> Original basis (purchase price)
> plus Capital Additions
> plus Costs of Sale
> less Cumulative Depreciation, Real Estate
> less Cumulative Depreciation, Capital Additions
> = Adjusted Basis

Fill in the data:

> 500,000 (Original basis (purchase price))
> plus 50,000 (Capital Additions)
> plus 38,500 (Costs of Sale)
> less 30,000 (Cumulative Depreciation, Real Estate)
> less 3,000 (Cumulative Depreciation, Capital Additions)
> = 555,500 (Adjusted Basis)

Answer 33-2:

You have a few interim calculations to perform before you use the formula. You made two capital additions, one for $40,000 and another for $30,000, so the total is $70,000. Accumulated depreciation on those additions is $5,100 and $1,500, for a total of $6,600. Your Costs of Sale are 7% of the $900,000 selling price, or $63,000.

Now use the formula.

800,000 (Original basis (purchase price))
plus 70,000 (Capital Additions)
plus 63,000 (Costs of Sale)
less 76,000 (Cumulative Depreciation, Real Estate)
less 6,600 (Cumulative Depreciation, Capital Additions)
= 850,400 (Adjusted Basis)

34

Depreciation

I f you own income-producing real estate, you can write off a portion of the cost basis of your asset each year That write-off is called deprecia-tion. With regard to real estate, the depreciable asset is the physical struc-ture or structures (i.e., the improvements), but not the land. Keep in mind that when you sell the property your accumulated depreciation deductions will be recaptured.

The cost of the asset is depreciated over the "useful life" of the asset. Under the tax rules at this writing, residential real estate has a useful life of 27.5 years, and non-residential 39 years.

You start depreciating when you place the property in service, but when figuring your actual depreciation allowance, you must also use something called a half-month convention. This means that the month you place the property in service, and also the month you dispose of the property, you may take only one half of the regular monthly amount of depreciation.

Depreciation Allowance (annual) = Depreciable Basis / Useful Life

Problem 34-1:

Several years ago you purchased an apartment building. At the time you acquired the property, the cost basis of the improvements was $550,000. What is your current year depreciation allowance?

Problem 34-2:

Last year you purchased a small shopping center for $1.4 million. 70% of the value lay in the building, and 30% in the land. What is your allowable depreciation this year?

Problem 34-3:

On July 1 of this year you purchased an apartment building for $1.7 million. According to the municipal tax assessor's records, the land was assessed for $350,000 and the building for $950,000. Did you overpay for the property? What is your allowable depreciation this year?

Answer 34-1:

You purchased the property several years ago, and it is fair to assume that you placed it into service when you purchased it. Since you didn't place it into service *this* year, the half-month convention is not applicable; you'll be taking a full year of depreciation.

The property is residential, so the useful life is 27.5 years.

Depreciation Allowance (annual) = Depreciable Basis / Useful Life

Depreciation Allowance (annual) = 550,000 / 27.5

Depreciation Allowance (annual) = 20,000

Answer 34-2:

You purchased the property last year, so once again the half-month convention is not in play.

70% of the $1.4 million cost is in the depreciable improvements.

1,400,000 x 0.70 = 980,000

The property is non-residential, so the useful life is 39 years.

Depreciation Allowance (annual) = Depreciable Basis / Useful Life

Depreciation Allowance (annual) = 980,000 / 39

Depreciation Allowance (annual) = 25,128

Answer 34-3:

At last you'll get to use the half-month convention. You purchased the property in July of this year, so you get to take one-half month of depreciation for July, plus five month's depreciation for August through December.

Start by estimating the percentage of the total property cost that is represented by the improvements. Using the relative valuation by the tax assessor is an approach you've used in previous examples. The land is assessed at $350,000 and the buildings at $950,000, so the total assessment is $1.3 million. The buildings represent what percentage of the whole?

950,000 / 1,300,000 = 73.1%

You paid $1.7 for the entire property and can reasonably estimate that 73.1% of that amount was for the depreciable improvements.

1,700,000 x 0.731 = $1,242,700

Now you can apply the depreciation formula for residential property to get the full annual allowance:

Depreciation Allowance (annual) = Depreciable Basis / Useful Life

Depreciation Allowance (annual) = 1,242,700 / 27.5

Depreciation Allowance (annual) = 45,189

However, you're not entitled to a full year of depreciation, but rather five and one-half months. Take the annual amount and divide by 12 to find the monthly amount. Then multiply the result by 5.5 to determine five and one-half months of depreciation.

45,189 / 12 = 3,765.75
3,765.75 x 5.5 = 20,712 (rounded)

Did you overpay for the property? Presumably the question is worth asking because the total tax assessment of $1.3 million is less than your purchase price of $1.7 million.

Remember from Chapter 32 that the assessment is not necessarily the same as the municipality's appraisal of the property's value. Many cities and towns assess based on a percentage of value, so you would use the techniques in Chapter 32 to back in to that appraised value.

Even if that appraised value is in fact lower than what you paid for the property, it still wouldn't be conclusive evidence that you had paid too much. Remember that an appraisal for assessment purposes may be several years old and not in sync with the current market. However, the relative values of land and buildings are likely to be useful longer than the appraisals themselves.

35

Gain on Sale

T he Gain on Sale is the profit you make when you sell a property. The gain is not merely the difference between what you paid for the property and what you sell it for. Rather it is the difference between the property's Adjusted Basis (see Chapter 33) and its selling price. You'll recall that the Adjusted Basis takes your original purchase price, increases it by Costs of Sale and cumulative capital additions, and decreases it by cumulative depreciation.

Anything that increases your Adjusted Basis reduces your taxable gain because it decreases the difference between the basis and the selling price. Anything that decreases your Adjusted Basis does the opposite, and increases your taxable gain.

Selling Price
less Adjusted Basis
= Gain on Sale

Problem 35-1:

You are selling a piece of real estate for $1 million. The property's adjusted basis is $750,000. What is your Gain on Sale?

Problem 35-2:

You are selling another property, also for $1 million. You originally purchased this parcel for $800,000. You have Costs of Sale of 7% and cumulative depreciation of $90,000. What is your Gain on Sale?

Problem 35-3:

You apparently have an inexhaustible supply of million-dollar properties, because you are about to sell yet another. You purchased this one for $735,000 and made $80,000 in capital additions to it. You have taken $42,000 in depreciation to date against the original improvements, and $6,000 in depreciation against the capital additions. It will cost you 6% of the selling price to accomplish the sale. What is your Gain on Sale?

Answer 35-1:

Apply the formula shown above to calculate the $250,000 gain.

Selling Price
less Adjusted Basis
= Gain on Sale

1,000,000 (Selling Price)
less 750,000 (Adjusted Basis)
= 250,000 (Gain on Sale)

Answer 35-2:

First you need the formula from Chapter 33 to figure the property's Adjusted Basis.

Original basis (purchase price)
plus Capital Additions
plus Costs of Sale
less Cumulative Depreciation, Real Estate
less Cumulative Depreciation, Capital Additions

= Adjusted Basis

800,000 (Original basis (purchase price))
plus 0 (Capital Additions)
plus 70,000 (Costs of Sale, 1,000,000 x 0.07)
less 90,000 (Cumulative Depreciation, Real Estate)
less 0 (Cumulative Depreciation, Capital Additions)
= 780,000 (Adjusted Basis)

Now use the formula for Gain on Sale:

Selling Price
less Adjusted Basis
= Gain on Sale

1,000,000 (Selling Price)
less 780,000 (Adjusted Basis)
= 220,000 (Gain on Sale)

Answer 35-3:

The procedure is the same as in Problem 35-2, except now you have more components to work with in your Adjusted Basis calculation.

735,000 (Original basis (purchase price))
plus 80,000 (Capital Additions)
plus 60,000 (Costs of Sale, 1,000,000 x 0.06)
less 42,000 (Cumulative Depreciation, Real Estate)
less 6,000 (Cumulative Depreciation, Capital Additions)
= 827,000 (Adjusted Basis)

Next, use the formula for Gain on Sale:

1,000,000 (Selling Price)
less 827,000 (Adjusted Basis)
= 173,000 (Gain on Sale)

36

Land Measurements

I n the United States, land is generally measured in acres or in square feet. There are 43,560 square feet in an acre. You can use these formulas to convert between acres and square feet:

Square Feet = Acres x 43,560

Acres = Square Feet x 0.000023, or Square Feet / 43,560

Countries that use the metric system usually measure land in hectares rather than acres.

Hectares = Acres x 0.4046854

Acres = Hectares x 2.471054

Problem 36-1:

You own a piece of land that is 23,500 square feet in area. How many acres is that?

Problem 36-2:

You own a parcel that is 0.77 acres in area. A little bird told you that it is worth $5 per square foot. Assuming the bird has the proper credentials to appraise raw land, what is the parcel worth?

Problem 36-3:

You contemplate building your retirement home in a temperate foreign principality and come upon a farmhouse for sale with 6.2 hectares of land. How many acres would you be buying? How many square feet?

Answer 36-1:

To convert square feet to acres, use one of the formulas shown above

Acres = Square Feet x 0.00023, or
       Square Feet / 43,560

Acres = 23,500 x 0.000023

Acres = 0.54

or

Acres = Square Feet / 43,560

Acres = 23,500 / 43,560

Acres = 0.54

Note that you will get more accurate results with the latter formula, because the 0.000023 factor unavoidably introduces some rounding error.

Answer 36-2:

First you need to convert acres to square feet.

Square Feet = Acres x 43,560

Square Feet = 0.77 x 43,560

Square Feet = 33,541

If the land is worth $5 per square foot, multiply to get the value, $167,705.

33,541 x 5 = 167,705

Answer 36-3:

First convert hectares to acres.

Acres = Hectares x 2.471054

Acres = 6.2 x 2.471054

Acres = 15.32

Then convert acres to square feet.

Square Feet = Acres x 43,560

Square Feet = 15.32 x 43,560

Square Feet = 667,339

Keep in mind again that the conversion factor from hectares to acres will introduce a small rounding error.

37

Building Measurements

B ecause you will typically rent commercial space by the square foot, it is important to have an understanding of how building area may be measured. In practice, the definitions of various measurements tend to be somewhat fluid; by lease agreement, you can choose to describe and define a space nearly any way you like. Nonetheless, the following definitions are typical:

Gross Building Area (GBA) – The total of all floors, including the basement

Usable Square Footage (USF) – The actual area occupied by a tenant or tenants, excluding common area

Rentable Square Feet (RSF) – Usually defined by lease, but often a tenant's USF plus an allocated share of common area

Loss Ratio = Common Area / Gross Building Area

Problem 37-1:

A commercial building measures 30 feet by 60 feet. It has six floors plus a basement. What is its approximate Gross Building Area?

Problem 37-2:

If the building in Problem 37-1 contains 2,520 square feet of common area, what is its loss ratio?

Problem 37-3:

A commercial building measures 60 feet by 90 feet and has eight floors plus a basement. It has 8,748 square feet of common area. The building is rented to two tenants. Each tenant occupies half of the Usable Square Footage. Each tenant's rent is based on its Rentable Square Feet, which is defined by lease as the tenant's Usable Square Footage plus 20% of the common area. The first tenant pays $22 per RSF per year, while the second tenant pays $24 per RSF per year. How much does each tenant pay per year in total dollars?

Answer 37-1:

With dimensions of 30' by 60', the building contains about 1,800 square feet per floor. There are six floors plus a basement, so 7 x 1,800 yields a Gross Building Area of 12,600 square feet.

Answer 37-2:

Use the formula,

Loss Ratio = Common Area / Gross Building Area

Loss Ratio = 2,520 / 12,600

Loss Ratio = 0.20, or 20%

Answer 37-3:

Start by calculating the Gross Building Area. The dimensions are 60' by 90', or 5,400 square feet per floor. The building has eight floors plus a basement, so the GBA equals 9 x 5,400 or 48,600 square feet.

Next figure the Usable Square Footage, which is the GBA minus the common area.

USF = GBA less common area

USF = 48,600 less 8,748

USF = 39,852 square feet

Each tenant occupies half of the USF, so each occupies 39,852 / 2 or 19,926 square feet.

The Rentable Square Footage for each tenant is based on its USF plus 20% of the common area.

8,748 (common area sf) x 0.20 = 1,749.6 square feet of common area allocated to each tenant's RSF

For each tenant, Rentable Square Footage equals Usable Square Footage of 19,926 plus a 20% allocation of the common area, 1,749.6 square feet.

RSF = USF + Allocation of common area

RSF = 19,926 + 1,749.6

RSF = 19,926 + 21,675.6 square feet

Finally, calculate the rent for each tenant. The first will pay $22 per square foot per year.

Rent = 21,675.6 RSF x $22 per RSF

Rent = $476,863 per year

The second tenant will pay $24 per square foot.

Rent = 21,675.6 RSF x $24 per RSF

Rent = $520,214 per year

Part Two

Case Studies

38

The Single-Family House

Many real estate investors, especially those who are just starting out, gravitate to single-family properties.

Throughout this book so far you've been serenaded with tales of apartment building and office building and shopping center investments. But the single-family is the square peg in our story. How is it different and why do people buy it as an investment?

Let's take the second question first. There have probably been no formal studies on this question, but this writer has some opinions on the subject and it was, of course, to hear such opinions that you bought this book.

Familiarity is surely the first and main reason. You probably already own a single-family house, and perhaps you grew up in one. You believe that you at least understand this type of property; you've gone through the financing drill and the closing. You feel more comfortable with what you know.

For some people, the opportunity to lust after quick riches may provide a second and compelling motivation. You've heard stories and seen books and infomercials about regular folks just like you and me who have bought a house and "flipped" it in days or weeks, making tens of thousands of dollars in profit. And then they did it again. Buy it before breakfast, sell it before lunch.

A lot of people made a lot of money doing this. Eventually, a lot of people also lost a lot of money doing this. You probably didn't hear as much from the latter because they didn't get as many book deals.

Flipping is a form of speculation, predicated on the assumption that property values are going to rise, often spectacularly. Many flippers think that home prices always go up, everywhere – or at least they thought so until about 2007. When speculators take over a market, sooner or later bad things are going to happen. If the rise in values in a particular location is driven by speculation rather than by the underlying economics of the community, eventually the music is going to stop and there are going to be very few chairs left. This is not investing.

You should recognize that investing is a program for the long-term building of wealth, and it has little or nothing to do with speculation.

Let's assume now that you have taken these warnings to heart, have avoided any area touched by speculators, and still wish to invest in and rent out a single-family house, a nice property nestled among a neighborhood of owner-occupied homes. How do you go about evaluating this property's investment potential?

You should start out by being aware that there are a few characteristics of single-family properties that differentiate them from apartment buildings, office buildings, shopping centers and other more typical income-producing properties.

One of these characteristics is density, or really the lack of it – specifically, the relationship between the number of rental units and the cost of the land. Say that you buy a ten-unit apartment building. It sits on a piece of land, and you apportion the cost of that land over 10 rent-producing units. If you buy a one-family house, you apportion the cost of the land over just one rental unit.

Obviously this is an oversimplification. The cost of the land isn't necessarily the same between the two properties. Then again, the single-family lot could easily be *more* expensive than the parcel on which the apartment building sits. Oversimplification or not, a general alert is in order. You may have a difficult time earning enough rent income from just one unit to carry the cost of the land as well as the building, since that cost per unit may be disproportionately high. In short, don't be terribly surprised if you have a hard time getting a positive cash flow from a single-family house used as a rental property. In contrast, a single condominium unit, which in most respects behaves like a single-family house investment, may disperse the cost of the land across a greater number of units.

A second and very important characteristic of this type of rental property investment is that its value is not likely to be a function of its ability to produce rent.

If the other houses in the neighborhood are being bought and sold as personal residences, then the prices in that community will be driven by the market for such residences, not by potential rental income. In other words, when you buy this property you will pay a price based on what people are paying for homes in the area; and when you sell it you can expect a price driven by that same market.

The market data approach to value is based on comparable sales. You can reasonably expect that a property will sell for something close to the price of similar properties located near the subject, i.e., comparables located in the same market. You would of course make adjustments for distinguishing features — the presence or absence of certain amenities found in the comparable properties — but it is the local market as much if not more than the property itself that drives the value.

There is a related characteristic that differentiates the single-family house from other income-property investments. When a property's value is a function of its income stream (as with typical commercial properties, apartment buildings, etc.), then you as an investor have the opportunity to create value by enhancing that income stream. You might be able to impose management improvements that allow you to enjoy higher rental income and less vacancy. Your active and inspired management increases the property's Net Operating Income and hence its value. You create equity.

On the other hand, if you purchase a single-family house for investment, you may be able to increase its value by making physical improvements, but you can't raise its value by improving its NOI. And in the back of your mind you know that those physical improvements might not return more than they cost, and they might not even survive cohabitation with tenants.

The difference, then, is in the degree to which you can personally influence the ultimate success of your investment. With a conventional income property you can have an impact on value, but with a single-family you must usually rely on general market conditions, over which you have little influence.

Even though the price at which you buy and the price at which you sell will not be a function of the property's rental income, you can still perform cash flow and resale projections, still estimate your rate of return, and still make a judgment as to whether or not this looks like it will be a successful investment.

The house may not be an income property in the purest sense, but that is how you're using it. You're buying an income stream and you need to estimate how much you can expect in the way of yearly cash flows and how much you'll derive from the final cash flow, the proceeds of sale. That's what investment analysis is all about. Let's see how it's done.

The Facts:

On January 1, 2011 you plan to close on the purchase of a 1,900 square foot single-family house for $179,000 with a 20% down payment. Your mortgage has a fixed rate of 6.75% for 30 years.

According to the tax assessor, 75% of the value of this property lies in the building and 25% in the land.

You believe it will take you two months to find a tenant who will pay $1,200 per month. During those two months you plan to go in and spend $1,800 on paint and some minor repairs to get the place looking good. You plan to budget $600 for repairs in the second year, and to increase that budget by 3% each year thereafter.

You assume that you'll be able to raise the rent in subsequent years, and figure that a 3% annual bump will probably be close to the increase in the overall cost of living.

The tenant will arrange for and pay all of his own utilities, including water. However, you decide that you don't want to rely on your tenant to cut the grass or shovel snow from the sidewalk – if he doesn't do it, the place will look like a disgrace – so you keep that responsibility for yourself. You budget for five snowstorms at $35 each and 12 lawn cuts at $20 each, and you assume that this expense will go up by about 5% per year.

Annual property taxes are currently $2,300 and have been rising at about 4% per year. Property insurance will cost you $900, and to be conservative you estimate that it will cost you 5% more each year.

You would like to keep the property for no more than five years. The biggest unknown, of course, is what will it be worth then? You decide to role-play several different possibilities. What if home prices stay flat for five years? What if they go up 3% per year? 6% per year? When you sell, you assume it will cost about 7% for the services of a broker and attorney.

One scenario you won't test is the possibility that values will decline. It's not impossible for that to happen, of course, but you certainly don't need to go through the exercise of an investment analysis to tell you that you would lose money.   If you thought the value of this property was headed down, you wouldn't (or certainly shouldn't) be buying it. You believe that the worst-case scenario for this market at this time is a flat five years.

You want to estimate your rent and expenses over time, as well as your cash flow. You want to see how well you'll do if you sell at the end of five years. But what if you have a family emergency? Could you bail out after two or three years without losing money?

You have a lot to think about.

Since this is your first detailed exercise, I must tell you in the spirit of full disclosure that for each case study I'm going to use one or another of my company's software products to perform the analysis and display the results to you, sometimes with exhibits trimmed down a bit to eliminate issues not dealt with in the problem. That doesn't mean you have to use those products too. You can use a pencil and paper and calculator, or you can build a spreadsheet to work with just the facts of the problem, or use some other software application, or take whatever approach suits you. The main focus here will not be, as in the first half of the book, on how to do the math, although you'll still see your share of numbers. And it will not be on how to run a particular software program. It will be about how to look at and think about the results.

The Analysis:

Let's begin by looking at the Annual Property Operating Data, extended over five years.

	2011	2012	2013	2014	2015
INCOME					
Gross Scheduled Rent Income	14,400	14,832	15,277	15,735	16,207
TOTAL GROSS INCOME	14,400	14,832	15,277	15,735	16,207
VACANCY & CREDIT ALLOWANCE	2,400	0	0	0	0
GROSS OPERATING INCOME	12,000	14,832	15,277	15,735	16,207
EXPENSES					
Insurance (fire and liability)	900	945	992	1,042	1,094
Lawn/Snow	415	436	458	481	505
Repairs and Maintenance	1,800	600	618	637	656
Taxes					
Real Estate	2,300	2,392	2,488	2,588	2,692
TOTAL EXPENSES	5,415	4,373	4,556	4,748	4,947
NET OPERATING INCOME	6,585	10,459	10,721	10,987	11,260

What is this APOD telling you about the investment? First and most striking is that you'd better keep your expectations in check during the first year. You anticipate losing two months' rent and plan to spend about three times your normal budget for repairs and maintenance, leaving your 2011 NOI depleted.

Things look a little better thereafter. Or do they? Remember our discussion above, about how the value of a single-family house would probably not be a function of its ability to produce income. Clearly, that seems true here. After the atypical first year, the property's NOI stabilizes in the $10k to $11k range. If you apply a 10% capitalization rate to those NOIs you would get a value estimate between $100,000 and $110,000, quite different from your $179,000 purchase price. (Although 10% may not be precisely the right rate for this market, cap rates have historically clustered between 8% and 12%, so 10% is a nice round number for making a rough estimate, and it has the advantage of allowing you to do the math in your head.)

As you begin to clutch your chest and tumble to the floor, you recall that whoever buys this property from you in the future will also pay based on its value as a home and not on its capitalized income. So, while the NOI would typically be very important to you as a determinant of value with other types of income property, with the single-family house its main significance is as a stepping stone to your calculation of cash flow.

Another issue that jumps off the page is that of vacancy and credit loss. You expect to lose two months' rent while you're getting the house ready, but you've made no provision for any future loss.

You decide to assume that a tenant who rents an entire house is likely to be less transient than someone who rents an apartment. Still, it's also reasonable to estimate that you'll have at least one turnover in five years and be at risk for some vacancy at that time. Let's modify the APOD to estimate the loss of one month's rent in the fourth year.

	2011	2012	2013	2014	2015
INCOME					
Gross Scheduled Rent Income	14,400	14,832	15,277	15,735	16,207
TOTAL GROSS INCOME	14,400	14,832	15,277	15,735	16,207
VACANCY & CREDIT ALLOWANCE	2,400	0	0	1,311	0
GROSS OPERATING INCOME	12,000	14,832	15,277	14,424	16,207
EXPENSES					
Insurance (fire and liability)	900	945	992	1,042	1,094
Lawn/Snow	415	436	458	481	505
Repairs and Maintenance	1,800	600	618	637	656
Taxes					
Real Estate	2,300	2,392	2,488	2,588	2,692
TOTAL EXPENSES	5,415	4,373	4,556	4,748	4,947
NET OPERATING INCOME	6,585	10,459	10,721	9,676	11,260

Your next step should be to estimate the property's taxable income or loss.

	2011	2012	2013	2014	2015
GROSS INCOME	14,400	14,832	15,277	15,735	16,207
- Vacancy & Credit Allowance	2,400	0	0	1,311	0
- Operating Expenses	5,415	4,373	4,556	4,748	4,947
NET OPERATING INCOME	6,585	10,459	10,721	9,676	11,260
Capitalization Rate	3.68%	5.84%	5.99%	5.41%	6.29%
Debt Coverage Ratio	0.59	0.94	0.96	0.87	1.01
- Interest, 1st Mortgage	9,618	9,513	9,399	9,277	9,148
- Depreciation, Real Property	4,678	4,882	4,882	4,882	4,882
- Depreciation, Capital Additions	0	0	0	0	0
TAXABLE INCOME OR (LOSS)	(7,711)	(3,936)	(3,560)	(4,483)	(2,770)

It looks like you can expect a tax loss for each of the next five years. Depreciation, a non-cash item, accounts for almost all of that tax loss. You will probably be able to use the loss to offset other ordinary income, so you have no problem with that.

You also notice that you were fortunate you didn't have to get commercial financing for this property. With a going-in Debt Coverage Ratio (see Chapter 23) of 0.59 you would have been substantially below the 1.20 threshold that most commercial lenders look for.

Of course, a DCR below 1.00 also implies that you're not taking in enough cash to cover your debt payments, which doesn't sound promising.

Now you're ready to move to the next step, which is your projection of cash flows. You'll recall from Chapter 13 that Cash Flow Before Taxes starts with Net Operating Income and is reduced by debt service and any capital additions or improvements. Since you made no improvements, the calculation of cash flow is straightforward.

	2011	2012	2013	2014	2015
NET OPERATING INCOME	6,585	10,459	10,721	9,676	11,260
- Debt Service, 1st Mortgage	11,145	11,145	11,145	11,145	11,145
CASH FLOW BEFORE TAXES	(4,560)	(686)	(424)	(1,469)	115
Cash on Cash Return (CFBT/Initial invest.)	-12.74%	-1.92%	-1.18%	-4.10%	0.32%
Cumulative Cash Flow Before Taxes	(4,560)	(5,246)	(5,670)	(7,139)	(7,024)

You girded your loins to expect a weak first year, because you needed to spend money on fix-up and you lost two months' rent. You still come up short in the next three years, however, finally breaking into positive territory, though not by very much, in the fifth year.

You should remember that you also had a tax loss each year. For simplicity, assume that you are in the 25% marginal tax bracket and are eligible to use all of those losses to offset other income. Your Cash Flow After Taxes looks a little more comforting.

	2011	2012	2013	2014	2015
CASH FLOW BEFORE TAXES	(4,560)	(686)	(424)	(1,469)	115
- Income Tax	(1,928)	(984)	(890)	(1,121)	(693)
CASH FLOW AFTER TAXES	(2,632)	298	466	(348)	808

Still, this is not a lot to show for a cash investment of 20%, or $35,800. For this investment story to have a happy ending, you'll need a very nice payday when you sell the property.

It should come as no surprise that if you project zero growth in the value of the property, this tale is bound to end like a Shakespearean tragedy, the stage littered with the dead bodies of all the main characters. Well, perhaps not quite that bad, but it still isn't going to be pleasant. Take a look at what happens.

	2011	2012	2013	2014	2015
PROJECTED SELLING PRICE	179,000	179,000	179,000	179,000	179,000
Selling Price Based on Appreciation Rate of 0.00%					
ORIGINAL BASIS, Purchase Price	179,000	179,000	179,000	179,000	179,000
+ Closing Costs, Amortized	0	0	0	0	0
+ Cumulative Capital Additions	0	0	0	0	0
+ Costs of Sale	12,530	12,530	12,530	12,530	12,530
- Adjusted Cumulative Depreciation	4,475	9,357	14,239	19,121	24,003
- Adjusted Cumul. Depr., Capital Add.	0	0	0	0	0
ADJUSTED BASIS AT SALE	187,055	182,173	177,291	172,409	167,527
GAIN OR (LOSS) ON SALE	(8,055)	(3,173)	1,709	6,591	11,473
TOTAL FEDERAL TAX ON SALE	(701)	(699)	478	1,699	2,919
PROJECTED SELLING PRICE	179,000	179,000	179,000	179,000	179,000
- Costs of Sale	12,530	12,530	12,530	12,530	12,530
- 1st Mortgage Payoff	141,673	140,041	138,295	136,427	134,430
BEFORE-TAX SALE PROCEEDS	24,797	26,429	28,175	30,043	32,040
- Total Federal Tax on Sale	(701)	(699)	478	1,699	2,919
AFTER-TAX SALE PROCEEDS	25,498	27,128	27,697	28,344	29,121
Internal Rate of Return, Before Tax	-43.47%	-21.33%	-12.86%	-9.30%	-6.00%
Modified IRR, Before Tax	-43.47%	-19.96%	-12.07%	-8.74%	-5.40%
Internal Rate of Return, After-Tax	-36.13%	-16.07%	-9.78%	-7.17%	-4.72%
Modified IRR, After-Tax	-36.13%	-15.41%	-9.43%	-6.87%	-4.41%
PV, NOI & Reversion	157,323	152,209	147,756	142,995	139,650
PV, CFAT and Sale Proc. After Tax	20,787	24,933	25,603	25,451	27,208
EQUITY, excluding reserves	37,327	38,959	40,705	42,573	44,570
RETURN ON EQUITY (CFBT/equity)	-12.22%	-1.76%	-1.04%	-3.45%	0.26%

There is scarcely any respite from the drumbeat of unwelcome news here. You can examine the various metrics, but if your purpose is to make a decision, you need look no further than the line, "After-Tax Sale Proceeds." In a situation where the growth in value over time is zero, at no point do you walk away from a sale with as much cash as you put in. Your initial investment was $35,800; the most you can hope to recoup is $29,121. A strong cash flow from operating the property might have taken away some of the sting of a disappointing sale, but as you saw above, your cash flow is dreadful, too.

Fortunately, this property does at least present you with some educational value, if no other kind. It gives you the chance to practice several of the concepts and calculations discussed in the first half of the book: Adjusted Basis (Chapter 33), Gain on Sale (Chapter 35), Sale Proceeds (Chapter 15), Internal Rate of Return (Chapter 19), Present Value (Chapter 4) and Return on Equity (Chapter 25). The math still works, even if you don't like the answers.

Clearly, this worst-case scenario is unacceptable. You also wanted to look at growth rates of 3% and 6%. Try 3% next. You can narrow your focus a bit and look at just the cash proceeds and the rate of return measures.

	2011	2012	2013	2014	2015
PROJECTED SELLING PRICE	184,000	190,000	196,000	202,000	208,000
- Costs of Sale	12,880	13,300	13,720	14,140	14,560
- 1st Mortgage Payoff	141,673	140,041	138,295	136,427	134,430
BEFORE-TAX SALE PROCEEDS	29,447	36,659	43,985	51,433	59,010
- Total Federal Tax on Sale	(701)	1,815	4,267	6,603	8,940
AFTER-TAX SALE PROCEEDS	30,148	34,844	39,718	44,830	50,070
Internal Rate of Return, Before Tax	-30.48%	-5.93%	2.10%	4.98%	7.01%
Modified IRR, Before Tax	-30.48%	-5.39%	2.19%	4.94%	6.85%
Internal Rate of Return, After-Tax	-23.14%	-4.53%	1.79%	4.26%	6.07%
Modified IRR, After-Tax	-23.14%	-4.25%	1.85%	4.28%	6.03%
PV, NOI & Reversion	161,550	160,663	159,635	157,605	156,396
PV, CFAT & Sale Proc. After Tax	25,015	31,947	36,531	40,438	46,253
EQUITY, excluding reserves	42,327	49,959	57,705	65,573	73,570
RETURN ON EQUITY (CFBT/equity)	-10.77%	-1.37%	-0.73%	-2.24%	0.16%

Things have looked so bad up to this point that almost any improvement seems like a victory. It appears that a sale somewhere between years two and three will at least let you recover your initial investment. That answers one of your questions above. Yes, you could bail out early in the event of an emergency and get your cash back, provided property values rise at least 3%.

Of course, simply not losing your shirt doesn't impress you as a very worthwhile investment goal. Your original plan was to make money. According to these projections, if you hold on through four or five years you should achieve an IRR in the range of 4% to 6% after taxes. Surely, that's looking better than what you saw before. However, most experienced real estate investors would probably tell you that you should require a greater IRR to balance the risks and uncertainties inherent in real estate investing. See if a 6% appreciation rate for this particular property will justify your risk-taking.

	2011	2012	2013	2014	2015
PROJECTED SELLING PRICE	190,000	201,000	213,000	226,000	240,000
- Costs of Sale	13,300	14,070	14,910	15,820	16,800
- 1st Mortgage Payoff	141,673	140,041	138,295	136,427	134,430
BEFORE-TAX SALE PROCEEDS	35,027	46,889	59,795	73,753	88,770
- Total Federal Tax on Sale	593	3,976	7,429	11,067	14,892
AFTER-TAX SALE PROCEEDS	34,434	42,913	52,366	62,686	73,878
Internal Rate of Return, Before Tax	-14.90%	7.41%	13.75%	15.56%	16.58%
Modified IRR, Before Tax	-14.90%	7.23%	13.30%	15.09%	15.93%
Internal Rate of Return, After-Tax	-11.17%	6.25%	11.69%	13.50%	14.61%
Modified IRR, After-Tax	-11.17%	6.18%	11.51%	13.31%	14.37%
PV, NOI & Reversion	166,623	169,118	171,513	172,850	174,875
PV, CFAT & Sale Proc. After Tax	28,911	39,283	48,029	56,671	67,896
EQUITY, excluding reserves	48,327	60,959	74,705	89,573	105,570
RETURN ON EQUITY (CFBT/equity)	-9.44%	-1.13%	-0.57%	-1.64%	0.11%

Now this property is starting to look like it makes some sense. You would do poorly if you sold at the end of the first year. In general you expect that to be true, because you have had little time to grow its value in one year but must still absorb the entire cost of sale. By the second year you're seeing modest returns, and thereafter you have a double-digit IRR – the kind of return that justifies the risks of investing in real estate.

The purpose of this type of analysis is to help guide you to a decision. So far you've examined the consequences of playing "What if…?" with one variable – the rate of price appreciation for single-family houses in your particular market. You've looked at worst-case and best-case scenarios, as well as half-way in between, or what you might call "most-likely." Worst-case proved unacceptable and most-likely was marginal. Do you really want to invest in a situation whose success depends on meeting your highest expectations?

Before you abandon this potential investment entirely, it's worth repeating that, in making your pro-forma projections, you've dealt only with the impact of one variable: appreciation rate. Even though this is a relatively simple analysis, there are a number of other variables that you could test to see how they impact the potential success of this investment. What if you purchased for a lower price?

What if your mortgage rate were lower but variable? What if your expenses grew faster or slower than you originally predicted?

If this were a real deal and you were investing real money, you might want to test the effect of each of these variables. (Let me suggest that if you want to try a lot of variations, then eschewing your yellow pad and using professionally designed real estate investment software should prove far more efficient and less prone to error.)

For the sake of illustration, however, it should be enough to examine what happens when you revisit just one other variable. Let's say that you hold your appreciation rate constant at the "most-likely" figure of 3% and test the impact of changing the starting monthly rent amount.

Previously you assumed that you would start at $1,200 per month, but you're really going to make this place look nice and you're a very effective salesperson. What if you can start at $1,350 instead? Re-run the numbers and see what you get.

	2011	2012	2013	2014	2015
GROSS INCOME	16,200	16,686	17,187	17,703	18,234
- Vacancy & Credit Allowance	2,700	0	0	1,475	0
- Operating Expenses	5,415	4,373	4,556	4,748	4,947
NET OPERATING INCOME	8,085	12,313	12,631	11,480	13,287
Capitalization Rate	4.52%	6.88%	7.06%	6.41%	7.42%
Debt Coverage Ratio	0.73	1.10	1.13	1.03	1.19
- Interest, 1st Mortgage	9,618	9,513	9,399	9,277	9,148
- Depreciation, Real Property	4,678	4,882	4,882	4,882	4,882
- Depreciation, Capital Additions	0	0	0	0	0
TAXABLE INCOME OR (LOSS)	(6,211)	(2,082)	(1,650)	(2,679)	(743)

	2011	2012	2013	2014	2015
NET OPERATING INCOME	8,085	12,313	12,631	11,480	13,287
- Debt Service, 1st Mortgage	11,145	11,145	11,145	11,145	11,145
CASH FLOW BEFORE TAXES	(3,060)	1,168	1,486	335	2,142
Cash on Cash Return (CFBT/Initial	-8.55%	3.26%	4.15%	0.94%	5.98%
Cumulative Cash Flow Before Taxes	(3,060)	(1,892)	(406)	(71)	2,071

	2011	2012	2013	2014	2015
CASH FLOW BEFORE TAXES	(3,060)	1,168	1,486	335	2,142
- Income Tax	(1,553)	(521)	(413)	(670)	(186)
CASH FLOW AFTER TAXES	(1,507)	1,689	1,899	1,005	2,328

	2011	2012	2013	2014	2015
PROJECTED SELLING PRICE	184,000	190,000	196,000	202,000	208,000
- Costs of Sale	12,880	13,300	13,720	14,140	14,560
- 1st Mortgage Payoff	141,673	140,041	138,295	136,427	134,430
BEFORE-TAX SALE PROCEEDS	29,447	36,659	43,985	51,433	59,010
- Total Federal Tax on Sale	(701)	1,815	4,267	6,603	8,940
AFTER-TAX SALE PROCEEDS	30,148	34,844	39,718	44,830	50,070
Internal Rate of Return, Before Tax	-26.29%	-1.39%	6.50%	9.14%	10.99%
Modified IRR, Before Tax	-26.29%	-1.19%	6.44%	9.00%	10.78%
Internal Rate of Return, After-Tax	-20.00%	-1.06%	5.24%	7.58%	9.29%
Modified IRR, After-Tax	-20.00%	-0.97%	5.25%	7.53%	9.15%
PV, NOI & Reversion	162,914	163,559	163,966	163,168	163,218
PV, CFAT & Sale Proc. After Tax	26,037	33,212	37,834	41,668	47,635
EQUITY, excluding reserves	42,327	49,959	57,705	65,573	73,570
RETURN ON EQUITY (CFBT/equity)	-7.23%	2.34%	2.58%	0.51%	2.91%

What's different about this scenario? And what isn't?

You may be surprised to see that your sale proceeds, both before and after taxes, are exactly the same now as they were when you projected lower rent income along with a 3% rate of appreciation. As discussed earlier, the value of a typical single-family house is not a function of its ability to produce rental income, so the value *should* be independent of the rent. You assumed a given purchase price and a given rate of appreciation. If your assumptions are correct, then they and they alone will set the selling price at any future date. Likewise, the outstanding mortgage balance will not change when your rent income rises. Indeed, the entire top half of the last exhibit above, from Projected Selling Price through After-Tax Sale Proceeds should remain exactly the same even if you never rent out the property at all, but live in it yourself, or keep it vacant but in good repair.

The increased rent affects your taxable income and your cash flow. Not to belabor the point, with what we might call a commercial investment property (i.e., one that is bought and sold for its income stream), the increased revenue would also affect the property's value – but not so here.

The effect on your cash flow is not insignificant. You will enjoy a positive cash flow, both before and after taxes, every year after the first. By the time you get to the fifth year, it represents about a 6% return on your initial investment.

Understand that even though the value of this property is not based on its income stream, it is in fact the entire income stream – your initial investment, your periodic cash flows and your sale proceeds – that combine to make up your return. So it is not surprising that the improvement in cash flow is reflected in an improved Internal Rate of Return. By the fifth year, your IRR before taxes is cracking the double-digit threshold.

You'll notice that there are some other metrics shown in this report. Since there are other property types still to consider, let's leave those so there will be something left to talk about in the remaining chapters.

Even though you have worked with only two variables in this analysis – single-family appreciation rate and rental income – you can see how you have already refined your decision-making process. Are you comfortable with the idea of a 3% growth rate? Are you confident you can get $1,350 per month in rent? In a real-life situation you would almost certainly refine the process further, testing different growth rates for expenses, different financing terms and even a different purchase price. Predicting the future is a very inexact science, but weighing a variety of alternative scenarios is your best chance to recognize some of the possible outcomes and to make informed decisions about your investing.

By way of review, consider the key points of this chapter:

1. The single-family house seldom functions like a typical income property. Even if held for investment, it will sell at a price that is determined by the market for homes in your area, and not as a function of its income. This is true when you're buying and when you're selling.
2. The "appreciation" in value of a single-family home, if it indeed occurs, is driven by economic factors over which you generally have little or no influence.
3. You can and should perform a cash flow and resale analysis on any rental property, even if it not bought and sold as a conventional income-producing property.

4. Yearly cash flow from operating a property is important to every real estate investor, but it's only part of the story, especially with the single-family house. Consider the example above with 0% appreciation. It's unlikely that any realistic level of rent (and subsequent cash flow) could make that investment attractive. Even with 3% appreciation, a substantial increase in rent and cash flow was only able to lift the investment from very marginal to borderline acceptable. The moral of the story: You have to look at the *entire* income stream to make an informed decision about a potential investment.

39

The Single Family, Redeveloped

W hen is a single-family house not a single-family house? There may be a lot of potential answers to that question, but here is one that will suit the purpose of this chapter nicely: When a developer comes across a nice big Victorian house in an area that is zoned for office use as well as residential.

At one time this building was probably a gracious and stately residence. I can't speak for you, but personally I've had to let most of my servants go, even the footman. Chances are there is a limited audience for this property as a single personal residence, but much greater appeal as professional office space, perhaps combined with some apartments.

How do you make economic sense of such a property? It's really a two-step process, although the steps are intertwined. First you need to look at it as a development project, then as an income property over time.

The Facts:

You are looking to acquire this property on January 1, 2012. You've been crawling all over it with architects and contractors and believe that you will spend 12 months and $450,000 to develop the building into three office suites that will rent for $3,500 each per month, and two apartments that will rent for $2,000 each. You expect rents to rise at 3% per year and will allow 2% for possible vacancy and credit loss. The prevailing cap rate for professional office buildings in this neighborhood is 9%.

You expect the 12 months to be sufficient time to secure permits and zoning approval, to leap all other legal hurdles, and to complete construction – a presumption which may qualify this book for placement on the "fiction" shelf in your library, but assume it to be correct anyway.

The $450,000 includes all "hard costs," i.e. construction costs, and most "soft costs" such as architectural and engineering, course-of-construction insurance, permits, real estate taxes during development, etc., but it does not include the cost of financing during the construction period.

Once construction is complete, the assessor expects taxes on the renovated property to be $15,200, with the building then representing 75% of the total value of the property. At that time, property insurance will cost $5,000 for the first year of occupancy. You will have a variety of other operating expenses totaling $22,300 in the first year. You project that all operating expenses will rise by 3% per year.

You expect to be able to pre-lease the property, so rent will begin to flow as soon as you are done with construction. Tenants will pay their own utilities, except for water (which is on a single meter) and for common-area lighting, which is on a house electric meter, paid by you. These latter items are included in the "other operating expenses" mentioned above.

You have up to $400,000 cash to put into the deal. Your lender, who has a Debt Coverage Ratio requirement of 1.25, will finance up to 75% of the total cost to purchase and renovate. In other words, the lender's Loan-to-Value Ratio is 75%. You can draw on the construction portion of the funds during the 12 months. During construction you expect to have on average 90% of the total loan commitment outstanding at any given time, and you will pay interest only at 7%. Thereafter the loan will amortize over 20 years.

You consider the asking price for the property to have no relevance to your decision-making process. The project needs to make economic sense, and you will not pay a price that the project cannot sustain. You'll decide what you're willing to pay.

As of yet you haven't decided if you will sell the property immediately after construction and leasing are completed, or hold it as investment for five additional years.

The Analysis

Real estate development is an enormous topic in its own right; this chapter is not going to teach you all you need to know to become a developer. It is worthwhile, however, to take note that sometimes your interests may be served best by creating an income property rather than taking over one that already exists. The fairly elementary example in this chapter brings out a few of the issues that developers routinely deal with.

If you go ahead with this deal, you will devote your first 12 months to completing the development project. In many respects, it won't be much different from buying a piece of raw land and developing the office/apartment complex. Your challenge will be to integrate your plan of design into the existing structure, rather than designing and building from scratch. Still, you will have created an income property where none existed before.

It's common for developers to analyze a project using either a so-called "front-door" or "back-door" approach. The difference between these two approaches lies in what you consider to be the unknown variable. With the back door, you believe you know the rental rate that you can obtain for the space once it is built. You also know the cost of financing your project and what you consider to be an acceptable rate of return on your own equity investment. Blend this all together and what you're really saying is that you can anticipate the revenue stream and want to figure out the maximum total project cost that you can support with that revenue stream.

As its name suggests, the front-door approach is a bit more direct. In this case you believe you know the total project cost – your outlay for improvements and for the cost or value of the land. Now the unknown variable is the revenue stream. What rent must you generate in order to make this deal worthwhile?

In this deal, you presume to know what income the property can generate once the renovation is complete. You want to figure out what total project cost – what cost for acquisition and development – is justified to produce that income stream.

There are a number of ways you can go about this, but since this a back-door approach let's see what useful information you can back into. Start off by assuming you've already finished your development project and are now happily collecting rent. More specifically, calculate your first year's Net Operating Income.

Remember Chapter 9?

Gross Scheduled Income
less Vacancy and Credit Loss
= Gross Operating Income
less Operating Expenses
= Net Operating Income

You have three offices at $3,500 per month (totaling $10,500) and two apartments at $2,000 per month ($4,000), giving you a Gross Scheduled Income of $14,500 per month or $174,000 per year.

Vacancy and Credit Loss is specified above at 2% of Gross Scheduled Income, or $3,480. Your operating expenses include $15,200 in real estate taxes, $5,000 for insurance, and $22,300 for other expenses, making a total of $42,500. You can now calculate your first full year's NOI:

174,000 (Gross Scheduled Income)
less 3,480 (Vacancy and Credit Loss)
= 170,520 (Gross Operating Income)
less 42,500 (Operating Expenses)
= 128,020 (Net Operating Income)

You can revisit another earlier chapter, #31, Maximum Loan Amount.

Maximum Loan Amount = Net Operating Income / Debt Coverage Ratio / (Monthly Mortgage Constant x 12)

Now you're ready to back your way into the maximum loan you can expect from your lender. You just figured out the NOI; according to the problem, the DCR can be no less than 1.25; and the mortgage constant for the stated loan terms, using the table you saw in Chapter 31, is 0.00775299.

Monthly Mortgage Payment per $1 – Mortgage Constant

Years	7.000%	7.125%	7.250%	7.375%	7.500%	7.625%
20	0.00775299	0.00782820	0.00790376	0.00797967	0.00805593	0.00813254
21	0.00758472	0.00766091	0.00773747	0.00781439	0.00789166	0.00796929

Maximum Loan Amount = 128,020 / 1.25 / (0.00775299 x 12)

Maximum Loan Amount = 1,100,823 (round to $1.1 million)

Since the lender's maximum Loan-to-Value Ratio is 75%, you can transpose the formula from Chapter 26 to back into the highest price or appraised value that can get financed:

Lesser of Property's Appraised Amount or Actual Selling Price
= Loan Amount / Loan-to-Value Ratio

Lesser of Property's Appraised Amount or Actual Selling Price
= 1,100,823 / 0.75

Lesser of Property's Appraised Amount or Actual Selling Price
= 1,467,764 (round to $1.465 million)

To be conservative, round this down to $1.465 million. Presumably, this is the highest total cost to purchase the existing property and redevelop it into offices and apartments that would be acceptable to the lender. It remains to be seen if it would be acceptable to you.

Remember that you have $400,000 of your own cash available to put into the deal. If your total cost of this project is actually $1.465 million and you finance $1.1 million, you would need to use about $365,000 of that money.

Assume for a moment that $1.465 million is indeed a realistic value for the finished project. What does that tell you about the amount you should pay to acquire the house and land?

You can subtract the total of the project costs from the ultimate value of the finished product and presume that that amount is what the house and land are worth on Day 1, before you begin your efforts to convert them into an income property.

What then are your total project costs? The problem states that your hard and soft costs are going to be $450,000, exclusive of interest on your financing during development.

Assume that you'll be borrowing the entire $1.1 million. On Day 1 the lender will give you sufficient funds (net of your cash investment) to acquire the property, then advance you funds as necessary to pay construction and development costs. As stated above, during the first year your average utilization of the total loan commitment will be 90%.

Ninety percent utilization suggests that you'll need to draw most of the funds early in the project, certainly for acquisition and probably to cover architect's fees, legal costs, and initial materials.

Ninety percent of $1.1 million equals an average outstanding balance of $990,000. At 7% interest only, the interest cost for the first year would be about $69,300. Add that amount to your previous $450,000 estimate for a total project cost of $519,300. Right?

Not so fast. You forgot something. Two things, actually.

First, you've got about $365,000 of your own money tied up for one year in a project that doesn't generate any income. Most developers would impute the interest lost on this money as a development cost. $365,000 is a big chunk of cash, and you could have invested it in an existing income property, perhaps at 10%. That lost interest represents an additional $36,500 cost, so now you're up to $555,800.

Second, a developer might charge a development or project management fee for putting the project together and for providing ongoing oversight. The developer would certainly include such charges if there were co-investors involved who would benefit from the project. But even if you are doing this alone it is entirely reasonable to say that part of the cost of this project includes the value of your time and expertise – time you spend at zoning hearings, arranging financing, chasing no-show subcontractors, arranging inspections and generally ensuring that everything stays on track. 10%, or $55,580, does not seem unreasonable.

Now your total project cost is $611,380. Call it $611,000.

If the finished value of the project is possibly $1.465 million and $611,000 is the cost of development and construction, then the existing property would be worth the difference, $854,000. All of this is true if it turns out that the finished product is a viable income property at a total cost of $1.465 million. No matter what else happens, the basic development and construction costs aren't going to change, so if you decide that the income stream from the finished property doesn't justify a $1.465 million valuation, any reduction you impose must come by way of reducing the purchase price for the original property.

(Note that certain development soft costs such as loan interest, developer's fee and imputed interest can change if the purchase price of the property changes. That's because they are a percentage of the *total* project cost, which includes the purchase price.)

You can see now why it is important for you to take this property from the point of its completion, and perform the same kind of pro-forma analysis over time, into the future, as you did when you considered the purchase of existing income properties. At a given total cost, will this property be a good investment for you if you keep it? Will it be a good investment at this price to a new owner if you try to sell it instead?

It's time to build some financial projections, very much as you did in the previous chapter. The only significant difference is that you won't use appreciation rate as a determinant of value. This is no longer a single-family residence. It is a commercial income property and its value will be determined by its ability to produce an income stream.

What calculation have you learned that relates the income stream to value?   (A pause here while you think.)

That's right. Go back to Chapter 10 if necessary and look at capitalization rate. You can calculate cap rate when you know the value (or price) and the NOI; by transposing the formula you can estimate value when you know the NOI and the cap rate.

In this case, you've estimated a NOI of $128,020 and you believe that the correct cap rate for this market is 9%. If the value of this property is now indeed a function of its income stream – that is, if an investor would buy this from you as a true income property and not as the personal residence it was when you first saw it – then this formula should give you a good estimate of its value:

Value = Net Operating Income / Capitalization Rate

Plug in the NOI and cap rate:

Value = 128,020 / 0.09

Value = 1,422,444 (round to $1.425 million)

Not too shabby. That's only a $40,000 difference from your original estimate, and what's forty grand between friends?

The correct answer, of course, is that it's forty grand – and now your top price to purchase the property drops from $854,000 to $814,000.

If you end up buying the property at a price of $814,000, and your development and construction costs are $611,000, then your total cost for the project will end up at $1.425 million.

Those of you who have particularly sharp pencils will be quick to point out that a change in the total project cost from $1.465 million to $1.425 million will reduce some development soft costs, as mentioned earlier.

Refigure those costs for the $1.425 million option. If that is the total project cost, the lender will not give you more than 75% of that amount, or $1,068,750. At 90% average loan utilization, your 7% interest cost would drop to $67,331. Your cash required would also drop to $356,250, meaning that the imputed lost interest for one year would now be $35,625.

Finally, your developer's fee would also drop to 10% of the subtotal of the above, or $55,296.

  450,000 (Basic hard costs and soft costs)
  plus 67,331 (Loan interest)
  plus 35,625 (Imputed loss of interest on cash invested_
  = 552,956
  plus 55,296 (10% developer's fee)
  = 608,252 (Total development construction costs, round to $608,000)
You're going to pay $814,000 for the property, and spend $608,000 for development and construction, making your total project cost $1.422 million. Actual-

ly, that's about what it was when you capitalized the NOI, before you rounded it up to the nearest 5k.

Those readers who are really alert will notice that there is some circular logic lurking here. You have an urge to re-figure this yet again, because when the total project cost drops, you need a slightly smaller loan and slightly less cash.

The loan interest during the development period is based on the total project cost. But that loan interest is also part of the total project cost, so the dependency works both ways. If you kept refiguring this repeatedly – by a process called "iteration" – you'd find that the changes would get smaller and smaller each time until they became truly trivial. We won't try to do that here manually because it would fill up a lot of pages and not make a meaningful change in the results. Please note, however, that software exists to perform such calculations automatically.

Let's restate the deal as we now have it, rounding the loan amount down to the nearest $1,000:

814,000 (Purchase price of the existing property)
plus 608,000 (Development and construction cost)
= 1,422,000 (Total project cost)
less 1,066,000 (Loan amount)
= 356,000 (Cash investment)

Now you can run a cash flow and resale pro forma to see if this looks like a good investment over time.

Speaking of time, most of the pro-forma analyses in this book look at holding periods of up to five years. There is nothing magical about that number. It should be sufficient for you to get a sense of what's going on without imposing numerical overload. In analyzing real deals, you may very well choose to look at longer periods, as in fact you'll do in the last chapter when you consider a shopping center.

Start with projections of taxable income:

	2013	2014	2015	2016	2017
GROSS INCOME	174,000	179,220	184,596	190,134	195,838
- Vacancy & Credit Allowance	3,480	3,584	3,692	3,803	3,917
- Operating Expenses	42,500	43,775	45,089	46,442	47,835
NET OPERATING INCOME	128,020	131,861	135,815	139,889	144,086
Capitalization Rate	9.00%	9.27%	9.55%	9.84%	10.13%
Debt Coverage Ratio	1.29	1.33	1.37	1.41	1.45
- Interest, 1st Mortgage	73,817	71,983	70,017	67,910	65,649
- Depreciation, Real Property	26,207	27,346	27,346	27,346	27,346
- Depreciation, Capital Additions	0	0	0	0	0
TAXABLE INCOME OR (LOSS)	27,996	32,532	38,452	44,633	51,091

As you can see, you have more than cleared your lender's 1.25 hurdle for Debt Coverage Ratio in the first year, and that coverage improves every year thereafter. Also, it's no surprise that you have a 9% cap rate for the first year, since you backed your way into that value when establishing the purchase price.

Look next at your expected cash flow, both before and after taxes.

	2013	2014	2015	2016	2017
NET OPERATING INCOME	128,020	131,861	135,815	139,889	144,086
- Debt Service, 1st Mortgage	99,176	99,176	99,176	99,176	99,176
CASH FLOW BEFORE TAXES	28,844	32,685	36,639	40,713	44,910
Cash on Cash Return (CFBT/Initial investment)	8.10%	9.18%	10.29%	11.44%	12.62%
Cumulative Cash Flow Before Taxes	28,844	61,529	98,168	138,881	183,791
	2013	2014	2015	2016	2017
CASH FLOW BEFORE TAXES	28,844	32,685	36,639	40,713	44,910
- Income Tax	6,999	8,133	9,613	11,158	12,773
CASH FLOW AFTER TAXES	21,845	24,552	27,026	29,555	32,137

Cash flow appears robust, starting off before taxes at about 8% of your initial investment and climbing by more than a point each year.

	2013	2014	2015	2016	2017
PROJECTED SELLING PRICE	1,422,000	1,465,000	1,509,000	1,554,000	1,601,000
- Costs of Sale	99,540	102,550	105,630	108,780	112,070
- 1st Mortgage Payoff	1,040,641	1,013,448	984,289	953,023	919,496
BEFORE-TAX SALE PROCEEDS	281,819	349,002	419,081	492,197	569,434
- Total Federal Tax on Sale	(477)	(465)	15,568	31,706	47,284
AFTER-TAX SALE PROCEEDS	282,296	349,467	403,513	460,491	522,150
IRR, Before Tax	-12.74%	7.68%	14.23%	16.98%	18.28%
Modified IRR, Before Tax	-12.74%	7.65%	13.73%	16.01%	16.92%
IRR, After-Tax	-14.57%	5.61%	10.83%	13.16%	14.40%
Modified IRR, After-Tax	-14.57%	5.65%	10.61%	12.68%	13.67%
PV, NOI & Reversion	1,330,716	1,375,181	1,416,968	1,456,240	1,493,758
PV, CFAT & Sale Proc. After Tax	279,028	343,137	394,990	449,583	508,520
EQUITY, excluding reserves	381,359	451,552	524,711	600,977	681,504
RETURN ON EQUITY (CFBT/equity)	7.56%	7.24%	6.98%	6.77%	6.59%

With about $100,000 in Costs of Sale to reckon with, you're not surprised that you can't recover all of your cash investment if you sell at the end of the first year. Of course, there are situations where you might not need to pay for the services of a broker, and in such a case a quick sale might be much more attractive. For example, you could sell the property directly to one of the office tenants, in which case your Costs of Sale would probably be limited to legal fees.

By the second year, even with full Costs of Sale, you can recover almost all of your original cash. Meanwhile, you've enjoyed about $32,000 in cumulative cash flow, so you're in the black overall.

Look next at some of the investment metrics shown in the bottom half of the illustration. By the second year your Internal Return of Return is at least showing signs of life, approaching 8% before taxes.

Modified Internal Rate of Return (or MIRR, about which you can learn more in the second edition of my *Cash Flow* book) is a generally more conservative variant of IRR. It presumes that you may have to put money aside on Day 1, earning interest at a "safe rate," to offset future negative cash flows; and that you may be able to reinvest your property's positive cash flows at a more modest "reinvestment rate," rather than at the property's IRR.

This property anticipates no negative cash flows, so the first component of MIRR is not relevant here. As you can see, this property's MIRR is indeed a bit lower than its standard IRR, reflecting the effects of the more conservative assumption about the rate at which positive cash flows can be reinvested.

The difference here between the IRR and the MIRR, however, is small and almost certainly not enough to change any decision you might make about this investment.

Next you see two Present Value measurements. The first should remind you of Chapter 4, Present Value and Chapter 16, Discounted Cash Flow. Rather than taking the PV of the cash flows and sale proceeds, you're taking the PV of the NOI and gross selling price, or reversion.

This is an approach that a commercial appraiser might use. The rationale here is that you want to look at the Present Value of what the cash flow would be if there were no financing and no income taxes involved. Why? Because neither the sort of financing that you personally are able to secure, nor the tax bracket that you fall into have any bearing on what the property is really worth. Your financing and taxes may have a lot to do with how well this property performs for you as an investment, but not with the discounted value of its income stream.

In this case, since you feel that 9% is an appropriate cap rate at which to value the current NOI, it is reasonable for you to discount the entire income stream using that same 9%. Once again, the third year of this deal seems to be the charm. It is at that point that the discounted value of the entire income stream (the before-financing and before-tax income stream, that is) is just about worth what you paid for it. Here the PV is $1.417 million compared to your purchase price of $1.422. By the fourth year, the PV is higher than the purchase price, suggesting that, over a four-year holding period, the income stream is returning at a rate of better than 9%.

The next PV measurement presents more of an investment than an appraisal orientation, because it does indeed look at an income stream that includes the cash flows and sale proceeds after taxes.

Here you're weighing the discounted value of the after-tax cash flows you receive against the actual cash you invested. You invested $356,000. If you were to sell the property at the end of the second year you would come close – $343,000 – to earning back your investment in discounted dollars. Once again, however, Year 3 is when you turn the corner. If you sell then, the value of your cash flows and sales proceeds, discounted at 9%, is about $395,000, once again telling you that over three years you are achieving better than 9%.

Before you wrap up your deliberations on this project, take a look at some other variables you might want to consider. Up to this point, you've assumed that the value of the project at the end of a given year was based on capitalization of its Net Operating Income for that same year. It's not uncommon for sellers of income property to take the position that the end-of-year value should instead be based on the NOI for the upcoming 12 months. The rationale is that the buyer is not purchasing last year's income stream but rather the income stream that begins when his or her ownership begins. Obviously the seller only offers this argument when next year's NOI promises to be greater and results in a higher value.

Not surprisingly, buyers tend to argue the reverse when the current year's NOI is less than that projected for next year.

There is no universally right or wrong position in this argument; one can often make a credible case either way, and self-interest generally dictates which argument you find more compelling. If a neutral third-party were to examine the details of the transaction, that person might say that the "next-year NOI" position is defensible to the extent that next-year's NOI is certain. In other words, if the projection of a higher NOI were based entirely on rental rates already locked in on multi-year leases, your argument would be strong. If it were based on mere speculation as to how much rent you could charge next year for leases that are renewing, your argument would be weak. And of course, between those two extremes is an ample grey area that can provoke lively discussion between sellers and buyers.

It's easy enough to re-run your numbers to see the impact of using next-year's NOI as a determinant of value.

	2013	2014	2015	2016	2017
PROJECTED SELLING PRICE	1,465,000	1,509,000	1,554,000	1,601,000	1,649,000
- Costs of Sale	102,550	105,630	108,780	112,070	115,430
- 1st Mortgage Payoff	1,040,641	1,013,448	984,289	953,023	919,496
BEFORE-TAX SALE PROCEEDS	321,809	389,922	460,931	535,907	614,074
- Total Federal Tax on Sale	(477)	8,731	24,869	40,448	56,212
AFTER-TAX SALE PROCEEDS	322,286	381,191	436,062	495,459	557,862
IRR, Before Tax	-1.50%	13.08%	17.37%	19.06%	19.72%
Modified IRR, Before Tax	-1.50%	12.86%	16.68%	17.93%	18.23%
IRR, After-Tax	-3.33%	9.87%	13.39%	14.96%	15.68%
Modified IRR, After-Tax	-3.33%	9.79%	13.05%	14.36%	14.85%
PV, NOI & Reversion	1,367,404	1,409,623	1,449,283	1,487,205	1,522,771
PV, CFAT & Sale Proc. After Tax	315,717	372,241	424,851	481,664	541,283
EQUITY, excluding reserves	424,359	495,552	569,711	647,977	729,504
RETURN ON EQUITY (CFBT/equity)	6.80%	6.60%	6.43%	6.28%	6.16%

Now, at the end of Year 1, you can sell at what would have been the End-of-Year 2 price. Or, at EOY 2 you can sell for what you would otherwise have waited three years to receive.

Remember the time value of money? Your bigger paydays from the sale of the property are now each occurring a year sooner. The sooner you can get your money, the more valuable it is; hence the IRR and MIRR here are higher each year.

Notice also that the columns of numbers for years two through five in the earlier (current-year NOI) example did not simply slide over one year to the left. You observe that the sale proceeds and tax liability are not the same if you sell for $1.509 million at the end of Year 2 instead of Year 3. Why?

One reason is that your mortgage balance for each year doesn't change just because you sell for a higher price. If you had to wait until Year 3 to get $1.509 million you would have paid your mortgage down for another year, adding to your proceeds before tax. If you sell in Year 2 instead of Year 3 you haven't claimed as much depreciation so there is less depreciation to recapture, which accounts for the difference in tax liability.

Clearly, if you can accomplish a sale of this property based on next-year's NOI, the project is even more attractive. Still, your return is negative if you want to sell at the end of the first year because the Costs of Sale are too great to absorb.

A few pages ago we noted that those costs might not need to be so great. What if you developed this project with its ultimate sale pre-arranged? In other words, if you built it to suit one of the eventual occupants, who agreed in advance to buy it when complete. Or what if you leased it with an option to buy? Assuming that no broker was involved in any of these transactions, you might estimate your Costs of Sale to be 1% rather than 7%. Re-run the previous scenario one last time with this revised cost.

	2013	2014	2015	2016	2017
PROJECTED SELLING PRICE	1,465,000	1,509,000	1,554,000	1,601,000	1,649,000
- Costs of Sale	14,650	15,090	15,540	16,010	16,490
- 1st Mortgage Payoff	1,040,641	1,013,448	984,289	953,023	919,496
BEFORE-TAX SALE PROCEEDS	409,709	480,462	554,171	631,967	713,014
- Total Federal Tax on Sale	13,628	27,771	43,517	59,660	76,000
AFTER-TAX SALE PROCEEDS	396,081	452,691	510,654	572,307	637,014
IRR, Before Tax	23.19%	24.18%	23.80%	23.25%	22.66%
Modified IRR, Before Tax	23.19%	23.62%	22.77%	21.84%	20.95%
IRR, After-Tax	17.39%	18.89%	18.85%	18.62%	18.32%
Modified IRR, After-Tax	17.39%	18.58%	18.27%	17.80%	17.30%
PV, NOI & Reversion	1,448,046	1,485,828	1,521,282	1,555,256	1,587,075
PV, CFAT & Sale Proc. After Tax	383,418	437,838	493,284	552,167	613,900
EQUITY, excluding reserves	424,359	495,552	569,711	647,977	729,504
RETURN ON EQUITY (CFBT/equity)	6.80%	6.60%	6.43%	6.28%	6.16%

Clearly, you can now sell the property in any of the first five years and realize an excellent return.

Let's review what you did and learned in this chapter.

1. Although this property may have begun its life as a single-family residence, it ended up as an income property. Its value upon resale was determined by its income stream.
2. You learned about the "front-door" and back-door" approaches to evaluating a real estate development project. With the former, you believe you know the total project cost and you to try to determine the revenue the project must generate in order to support both that cost and your expected return. With the latter, as used in this case study, you believe you know what the revenue stream will be, as well as what you consider to be an acceptable rate of return. Your mission is to determine the

maximum total project cost that you can support with that revenue stream.

3. Because this was a development project and not the purchase and eventual resale of a single-family home you needed to take a different approach to estimating the price you would be willing to pay to acquire the property. That approach involved treating the acquisition as part of the total cost of a development project. In order to be feasible, the total project cost could not exceed what the finished property's income stream would justify.

4. In estimating the cost to develop the project, you took into account the cost of capital tied up during the development period (i.e., lost interest), as well as the value of the time and expertise you contributed (the development or project management fee.)

5. You figured the cost of development and construction financing using loan draws by estimating the average percentage of loan utilized during the development period.

6. You produced cash flow and resale projections to estimate the holding period needed to achieve an acceptable return.

7. You learned about the difference between Modified Internal Rate of Return and standard IRR. MIRR presumes that you may have to put money aside at a "safe rate," to offset future negative cash flows; and that you may be able to reinvest your property's positive cash flows at a more modest "reinvestment rate," rather than at the property's IRR.

8. You investigated the effect that estimating value based on next year's NOI, rather than the current year's NOI, would have on your rate of return and planned holding period.

9. You also investigated the impact of reducing your Costs of Sale by selling directly, without brokerage fees.

40

The Apartment Complex

S o far you have looked at two properties that presented special issues. The first was a standard single-family house being used as a rental property. The second was a single-family that you treated much as you would a piece of raw land, developing it into a small, mixed-use property.

Now you'll turn your attention to something that is a bit more conventional among income-property investments: an apartment building.

This should be a fairly straightforward analysis, but you can use it to perform some serious "What if...?" scrutiny. What if you buy the property at a better price? What if you secure more (or less) favorable terms for your financing? What if some of your expenses can be pared?

The Facts

Tranquil Manor is a 33,000 square foot apartment complex located at 100 Lois Lane, South Haven, CT. The location is fully built up and well established with multi-family housing. The prevailing capitalization rate in this area for properties such as this is 11%. You are contemplating the purchase of this property on January 1, 2014.

The building is brick, about 50 years old and has been well-maintained. There is no evidence of deferred maintenance or of the need to replace the roof or mechanicals at any time in the near future. 75% of the value of the property lies in the building and 25% in the land.

The building has 48 apartments. Every apartment is occupied and all leases expire within a year. The owner has presented you with the following rent roll information:

10 studio apartments @ $700 each
30 1-bedroom apartments @ $950 each
8 2-bedroom apartments @ $1,150 each

Your research shows that such rents are realistic in this market and also that rents have been increasing at about 2% per year. Although there are no vacancies now, you estimate a 2% allowance for uncollectible rent.

You combine the owner's representations with your knowledge of similar buildings and come up with the following estimate of first-year operating expenses:

Accounting	2,500
Insurance (fire and liability)	29,300
Lawn/Snow	7,400
Legal	6,200
Miscellaneous	3,200
Property Management	38,400
Repairs and Maintenance	29,300
Supplies	7,400
Real Estate Taxes	42,600
Trash Removal	18,600
Electricity	12,200
Sewer and Water	29,500
Telephone	800

You believe that each of these expenses will increase at 3% per year except insurance (5%) and real estate taxes (4%).

The seller's asking price is $3 million. You expect you can obtain financing for 70% of the purchase price. The loan terms include a 7% initial rate, 240-month term and two points. The rate will adjust annually and you project that it will increase 1% each year for the next two years, then remain stable. The lender requires a Debt Coverage Ratio no less than 1.20.

The seller will also take back secondary financing in the amount of $300,000. The terms are 8.5% initial rate, 120-month term and no points. The note calls for an annual rate adjustment; again you project 1% increases in the second and third years.

You expect to spend $10,000 in legal and related costs to close the transaction. You also expect to pay 7% of the selling price as your cost of sale when you eventually dispose of the property.

Begin your analysis of this property by constructing an APOD form (see Chapter 9) and extending it over five years. What is your projected Net Operating Income in the first year? Given the market's prevailing cap rate, does the asking price seem realistic?

Note that your NOI is going up each year, but at a decelerating rate. Why?

Next build a pro forma of the cash flows and potential resale over time, as you did in the previous two chapters.

What is your total cash investment in this deal?

What numbers will your first mortgage lender probably focus on? Are those numbers likely to be satisfactory?

Look at the Cash Flow Before Taxes. You notice that it declines over the first three years, then slowly recovers. Why?

Examine the projected selling price for each of the first five years. How do these projections compare to your original purchase price?

Look at the projected Gain on Sale, Sale Proceeds Before Taxes and Internal Rate of Return. Are you going to benefit from the sale of this property at any point during the first five years?

If you have been doing your work on a computer, save your efforts so far with a name like, "Original apartment case study."

Now start playing, "What if...?" Begin by reducing the purchase price $200,000 at a time; then reconsider the cash flow and resale questions above. Remember to adjust the financing so that it remains 70% of the purchase price.

If you leave all other assumption unchanged for now, at what price does the deal begin to look acceptable? At what price does it look so good, you start to tell stories about it to your golf partners? Keep in mind that there are no precisely correct answers to these questions. Think like an investor. What kinds of returns are acceptable to you?

Again, if you are using a computer, save one or more of these modified analyses (always with unique names) so you can get more creative and test some other scenarios. What if you convince the seller to accept a lower interest rate and/or longer term on the secondary financing? What if you can negotiate a lower-cost property management contract, perhaps with no increase for the second year? What if interest rates don't go up by a full point in years two and three? What if they go up more than one point, or if they go up every year? What if you find a lender willing to give you a 75% loan-to-value ratio? What if you are able to obtain an interest-only first mortgage at the same rate as the amortized loan? At 0.5% higher than the amortized loan?

Mix and match these changes along with variations in the purchase price to see how they impact the performance of this investment. Try some other changes as well to see if you can structure viable alternatives to the original proposition.

As you begin to test different possibilities and try to re-shape the transaction into one you can accept, you'll begin to appreciate the enormous power of this type of "What if...?" analysis.

The Analysis

Before you can begin your APOD (Annual Property Operating Data), you'll need to determine the property's Gross Scheduled Income. The facts above specify the current rents and to those you can apply the 2% annual increase for years two through five (2015- 2018).

	2014	2015	2016	2017	2018
10 studio apartments @ $700 ave.	84,000	85,680	87,394	89,142	90,925
30 1-bedroom @ $950	342,000	348,840	355,817	362,933	370,192
8 2-bedroom @ $1,150	110,400	112,608	114,860	117,157	119,500
Totals for Property	536,400	547,128	558,071	569,232	580,617

Now that you have the Gross Scheduled Income, you can create an APOD form. You need to impose a 2% allowance for vacancy and credit loss. The problem specifies the first-year amount for the operating expenses shown below, and tells you to assume that they will increase at 3% per year except insurance (5%) and real estate taxes (4%).

You've derived an expected Net Operating Income for each of the first five years.

	2014	2015	2016	2017	2018
INCOME					
Gross Scheduled Rent Income	536,400	547,128	558,071	569,232	580,617
TOTAL GROSS INCOME	536,400	547,128	558,071	569,232	580,617
VACANCY & CREDIT ALLOW.	10,728	10,943	11,161	11,385	11,612
GROSS OPERATING INCOME	525,672	536,185	546,910	557,847	569,005
EXPENSES					
Accounting	2,500	2,575	2,652	2,732	2,814
Insurance (fire and liab.)	29,300	30,765	32,303	33,918	35,614
Lawn/Snow	7,400	7,622	7,851	8,087	8,330
Legal	6,200	6,386	6,578	6,775	6,978
Miscellaneous	3,200	3,296	3,395	3,497	3,602
Property Management	38,400	39,552	40,739	41,961	43,220
Repairs and Maintenance	29,300	30,179	31,084	32,017	32,978
Supplies	7,400	7,622	7,851	8,087	8,330
Taxes					
Real Estate	42,600	44,304	46,076	47,919	49,836
Trash Removal	18,600	19,158	19,733	20,325	20,935
Utilities					
Electricity	12,200	12,566	12,943	13,331	13,731
Sewer and Water	29,500	30,385	31,297	32,236	33,203
Telephone	800	824	849	874	900
TOTAL EXPENSES	227,400	235,234	243,351	251,759	260,471
NET OPERATING INCOME	298,272	300,951	303,559	306,088	308,534

The "Facts" section above is sprinkled liberally with questions; let's re-state and try to address some of them.

Given the market's prevailing cap rate, does the asking price seem realistic?

The property's first-year NOI is $298,272 and the prevailing cap rate for this market is stated to be 11%. By now you know the drill from Chapter 10:

Value = Net Operating Income / Capitalization Rate

Value = 298,272 / 0.11

Value = 2,711,564

The seller's asking price is $3 million. $2.7 is what you think you can reasonably get for it at the end of your first year of ownership. Based on the information you have so far, it looks like the property may be overpriced by 10% or more.

Note that your NOI is going up each year, but at a decelerating rate. Why?

The NOI is essentially the difference between income and operating expenses. In this case your income begins at more than twice the amount of your expenses and is increasing at 2% per year. Most of your expenses are going up by 3% (except taxes and insurance at 4% and 5%, respectively), with the overall increase being close to 3.5%.

Your income is increasing by more dollars than your expenses in each of these first five years, so your NOI is going up. However, the *rate* of increase in expenses, about 3.5%, is greater than the 2% rate of increase in rent, so expenses are catching up gradually. Hence, the NOI is rising but by a smaller and smaller percentage each year because expenses are going up faster than income.

Next build a pro forma of the cash flows and potential resale over time, as you did in the previous two chapters.

First, the taxable income or loss:

	2014	2015	2016	2017	2018
GROSS INCOME	536,400	547,128	558,071	569,232	580,617
- Vacancy & Credit Allowance	10,728	10,943	11,161	11,385	11,612
- Operating Expenses	227,400	235,234	243,351	251,759	260,471
NET OPERATING INCOME	298,272	300,951	303,559	306,088	308,534
Capitalization Rate	9.94%	10.03%	10.12%	10.20%	10.28%
Debt Coverage Ratio	1.24	1.17	1.11	1.12	1.13
- Interest, 1st Mortgage	145,417	162,272	178,294	173,915	169,124
- Interest, 2nd Mortgage	24,737	25,724	26,205	23,797	21,122
- Depreciation, Real Property	78,758	82,182	82,182	82,182	82,182
- Depreciation, Capital Additions	0	0	0	0	0
- Amortization of Points, 1st Mort.	2,100	2,100	2,100	2,100	2,100
TAXABLE INCOME OR (LOSS)	47,260	28,673	14,778	24,094	34,006

Next, the Cash Flow Before Taxes:

	2014	2015	2016	2017	2018
NET OPERATING INCOME	298,272	300,951	303,559	306,088	308,534
- Debt Service, 1st Mortgage	195,375	210,212	224,983	224,983	224,983
- Debt Service, 2nd Mortgage	44,635	46,416	48,063	48,063	48,063
- Capital Additions	0	0	0	0	0
CASH FLOW BEFORE TAXES	58,262	44,323	30,513	33,042	35,488
Cash on Cash Return (CFBT/Initial invest.)	8.94%	6.80%	4.68%	5.07%	5.44%
Cumulative Cash Flow Before Tax	58,262	102,585	133,098	166,140	201,628

The Cash Flow After Taxes:

	2014	2015	2016	2017	2018
CASH FLOW BEFORE TAXES	58,262	44,323	30,513	33,042	35,488
- Income Tax	11,815	7,168	3,695	6,024	8,502
CASH FLOW AFTER TAXES	46,447	37,155	26,818	27,018	26,986

The projected selling price and gain:

	2014	2015	2016	2017	2018
PROJECTED SELLING PRICE	2,712,000	2,736,000	2,760,000	2,783,000	2,805,000
Selling Price Based on Capitalization Rate of 11.00%					
ORIGINAL BASIS, Purchase Price	3,000,000	3,000,000	3,000,000	3,000,000	3,000,000
+ Closing Costs, Amortized	10,000	10,000	10,000	10,000	10,000
+ Cumulative Capital Additions	0	0	0	0	0
+ Costs of Sale	189,840	191,520	193,200	194,810	196,350
- Adjusted Cumul. Depr., R. E.	75,334	157,516	239,698	321,880	404,062
- Adjusted Cumul. Depr. Cap. Add.	0	0	0	0	0
ADJUSTED BASIS AT SALE	3,124,506	3,044,004	2,963,502	2,882,930	2,802,288
GAIN OR (LOSS) ON SALE	(412,506)	(308,004)	(203,502)	(99,930)	2,712

Finally, the proceeds of resale and rates of return:

	2014	2015	2016	2017	2018
PROJECTED SELLING PRICE	2,712,000	2,736,000	2,760,000	2,783,000	2,805,000
- Costs of Sale	189,840	191,520	193,200	194,810	196,350
- 1st Mortgage Payoff	2,050,042	2,002,102	1,955,413	1,904,345	1,848,486
- 2nd Mortgage Payoff	280,102	259,410	237,552	213,286	186,345
BEFORE-TAX SALE PROCEEDS	192,016	282,968	373,835	470,559	573,819
- Total Federal Tax on Sale	(9,905)	(9,344)	(8,819)	(8,294)	(6,341)
AFTER-TAX SALE PROCEEDS	201,921	292,312	382,654	478,853	580,160
IRR, Before Tax	-61.61%	-24.54%	-8.89%	-0.67%	4.04%
Modified IRR, Before Tax	-61.61%	-22.70%	-7.35%	0.24%	4.44%
IRR, After-Tax	-61.91%	-25.26%	-9.64%	-1.55%	3.01%
Modified IRR, After-Tax	-61.91%	-23.74%	-8.32%	-0.70%	3.47%
PV, NOI & Reversion	2,540,930	2,578,129	2,611,754	2,641,482	2,667,768
PV, CFAT & Sale Proc. After Tax	223,755	296,817	368,894	455,740	546,978
EQUITY, excluding reserves	381,856	474,488	567,035	665,369	770,169
RETURN ON EQUITY (CFBT/equity)	15.26%	9.34%	5.38%	4.97%	4.61%

Let's return to the questions raised above.

What is your total cash investment in this deal?

This is not a trick question; you simply haven't made this calculation before. In real deals you will usually have to reach into your pocket for more than just the down payment. The first mortgage lender is providing 70% of the $3 million purchase price, or $2.1 million, and the seller is taking back a second mortgage of $300,000. That means you have a total of $2.4 million in financing, leaving you to come up with $600,000 as the down payment. However, the first mortgage also requires that you pay two points; 2% of $2.1 million is $42,000. You also have closing costs of $10,000, so your entire cash investment in this deal is $652,000.

What numbers will your first mortgage lender probably focus on? Are those numbers likely to be satisfactory?

The lender may look at the overall Loan-to-Value Ratio. Some lenders just want to be certain that they're not funding more than a given percentage of the property's value or selling price, but others may look askance if some of your "equity" is not equity at all but rather debt from another source.

The rationale here is obvious. The less money you have at risk, the greater the chance you might default if the property runs into hard times. That's why they have a Loan-to-Value requirement to begin with. If this lender has no problem with secondary financing then this is non-issue, but you should be aware of their underwriting policies before you begin the loan process.

The lender will certainly look at the Debt Coverage Ratio to see if you meet its 1.20 requirement. In the first year you hit 1.24, so you pass muster. In the second year you slip below the threshold, hitting only 1.17, and in the third year you slip even further to 1.11. Why is this happening? You'll find that one answer explains both this and your wavy cash flow.

Look at the Cash Flow Before Taxes. You notice that it declines over the first three years, then slowly recovers. Why?

Both the first and second mortgages have adjustable interest rates. You have assumed that each loan's rate will rise by a full percentage point in Year 2 and again in Year 3, but remain level thereafter. With the initial rate, the property is able to cover the debt service on the first mortgage well enough to satisfy the lender's DCR requirement. As the interest rate increases, so does the debt service. The higher debt service means the NOI is no longer able to cover the 1.20 DCR. It also means that your cash flow is reduced because more money is going to pay interest and less is left to go into your pocket.

Once the interest rate on both mortgages – and hence the debt service – levels off, the growing NOI slowly reverses this trend. There is gradually more cash available to cover the debt and to revive the cash flow.

Examine the projected selling price for each of the first five years. How do these projections compare to your original purchase price?

You can see from the figure above that the projected selling price, based on capitalization of the property's NOI, ranges from about $2.7 to $2.8 million over the first five years. So, even if you hold the property for five years, you doubt your ability to sell it for as much as you paid for it.

Look at the projected Gain on Sale, Sale Proceeds Before Taxes and Internal Rate of Return. Are you going to benefit from the sale of this property at any point during the first five years?

There is virtually no good news in these numbers. It is not until the fifth year that you see anything but a taxable loss upon sale – and the small gain in Year 5 is entirely a function of the fact that your accumulated depreciation has lowered your basis, so the anemic selling price is finally more than the basis.

Likewise, your expected sale proceeds are grim. Even after five years of ownership, you don't expect to get back your initial cash investment when you sell. Your IRR is negative through the first four years, turning just minimally positive in the fifth.

Begin by reducing the purchase price $200,000 at a time; then reconsider the cash flow and resale questions above. ...

If you leave all other assumption unchanged for now, at what price does the deal begin to look acceptable? At what price does it look so good, you start to tell stories about it to your golf partners?

Let's see how this looks if you reduce the purchase to $2.8 million.

	2014	2015	2016	2017	2018
NET OPERATING INCOME	298,272	300,951	303,559	306,088	308,534
- Debt Service, 1st Mortgage	182,350	196,198	209,984	209,984	209,984
- Debt Service, 2nd Mortgage	44,635	46,416	48,063	48,063	48,063
- Capital Additions	0	0	0	0	0
CASH FLOW BEFORE TAXES	71,287	58,337	45,512	48,041	50,487
Cash on Cash Return (CFBT/Initial invest.)	12.10%	9.90%	7.72%	8.15%	8.57%
Cumulative Cash Flow Before Tax	71,287	129,624	175,136	223,177	273,664

Your cash flow is better for one reason: Since you assume the amount of the first mortgage will be 70% of the purchase price, the amount of that mortgage is smaller and its debt service is less.

Now consider the resale and overall return:

	2014	2015	2016	2017	2018
PROJECTED SELLING PRICE	2,712,000	2,736,000	2,760,000	2,783,000	2,805,000
- Costs of Sale	189,840	191,520	193,200	194,810	196,350
- 1st Mortgage Payoff	1,913,373	1,868,628	1,825,052	1,777,388	1,725,254
- 2nd Mortgage Payoff	280,102	259,410	237,552	213,286	186,345
BEFORE-TAX SALE PROCEEDS	328,685	416,442	504,196	597,516	697,051
- Total Federal Tax on Sale	(9,294)	(8,771)	(8,281)	12,635	37,422
AFTER-TAX SALE PROCEEDS	337,979	425,213	512,477	584,881	659,629
IRR, Before Tax	-32.12%	-3.98%	5.43%	9.94%	12.36%
Modified IRR, Before Tax	-32.12%	-3.29%	5.60%	9.54%	11.51%
IRR, After-Tax	-33.18%	-5.62%	3.79%	7.48%	9.44%
Modified IRR, After-Tax	-33.18%	-4.99%	4.07%	7.43%	9.11%
PV, NOI & Reversion	2,540,930	2,578,129	2,611,754	2,641,482	2,667,768
PV, CFAT & Sale Proc. After Tax	354,671	425,476	495,427	560,902	628,286
EQUITY, excluding reserves	518,525	607,962	697,396	792,326	893,401
RETURN ON EQUITY (CFBT/equity)	13.75%	9.60%	6.53%	6.06%	5.65%

This is better than a purchase at $3 million, but hardly anything to get excited about. It's not until the fifth year that you can sell for the same price at which you purchased. Likewise, you must wait until Year 5 to recover your initial investment when you sell and to see a respectable IRR. You'll probably decide that $2.8 million is still more than you should pay for this property. What about $2.6 million?

	2014	2015	2016	2017	2018
NET OPERATING INCOME	298,272	300,951	303,559	306,088	308,534
- Debt Service, 1st Mortgage	169,325	182,183	194,985	194,985	194,985
- Debt Service, 2nd Mortgage	44,635	46,416	48,063	48,063	48,063
- Capital Additions	0	0	0	0	0
CASH FLOW BEFORE TAXES	84,312	72,352	60,511	63,040	65,486
Cash on Cash Return (CFBT/Initial invest.)	16.02%	13.74%	11.50%	11.98%	12.44%
Cumulative Cash Flow Before Tax	84,312	156,664	217,175	280,215	345,701

Once again a reduction in the price means a smaller first mortgage and less debt service. You're achieving a healthy cash flow despite the climb in the interest rates on your mortgages; cash-on-cash return stays in double digits.

	2014	2015	2016	2017	2018
PROJECTED SELLING PRICE	2,712,000	2,736,000	2,760,000	2,783,000	2,805,000
- Costs of Sale	189,840	191,520	193,200	194,810	196,350
- 1st Mortgage Payoff	1,776,703	1,735,154	1,694,691	1,650,432	1,602,021
- 2nd Mortgage Payoff	280,102	259,410	237,552	213,286	186,345
BEFORE-TAX SALE PROCEEDS	465,355	549,916	634,557	724,472	820,284
- Total Federal Tax on Sale	(8,684)	10,324	34,177	57,798	81,186
AFTER-TAX SALE PROCEEDS	474,039	539,592	600,380	666,674	739,098
IRR, Before Tax	4.42%	17.03%	19.68%	20.60%	20.87%
Modified IRR, Before Tax	4.42%	16.34%	18.19%	18.51%	18.34%
IRR, After-Tax	2.39%	12.81%	14.96%	15.85%	16.24%
Modified IRR, After-Tax	2.39%	12.49%	14.19%	14.71%	14.80%
PV, NOI & Reversion	2,540,930	2,578,129	2,611,754	2,641,482	2,667,768
PV, CFAT & Sale Proc. After Tax	485,590	537,450	584,195	644,231	709,593
EQUITY, excluding reserves	655,195	741,436	827,757	919,282	1,016,634
RETURN ON EQUITY (CFBT/equity)	12.87%	9.76%	7.31%	6.86%	6.44%

At last you're getting somewhere. The first year is still unappealing, but you're getting used to seeing that in most of your analyses. The cost of selling a property immediately after you've purchased it tends to drain any hope of a return.

Your projected selling price after one year, however, is at last more than you paid for the property – and it continues to rise each year. Your actual purchase price is finally starting to look like the Present Value of the NOI and Reversion, discounted at 11%. Remember that this calculation is the commercial appraiser's approach to value – it's the present worth of the future income stream, discounted at a particular rate of return. Since 11% is the prevailing cap rate among properties of this type in this location, you judge this to be the appropriate rate to use. Looking at the result of this calculation, you begin to think that perhaps $2.54 million might be the price you want to aim for.

Examining your return on investment, as expressed by the IRR and MIRR, also lifts your spirits. These numbers are now starting to look like something you could live with.

Is the deal now so good that you ready to brag to your golf buddies? Not yet. I'll leave it to you to decide how far down you need to get the price before this deal achieves the status of urban legend.

At the end of "The Facts," above, I suggested that you try a number of other variations as to how you might structure this deal, such as the use of different financing terms. I won't attempt to display the results of so many permutations, but you should try some of them independently to gain a sense of the power that "What if…?" analysis can give you in structuring your deals.

The Truth Comes Out

Now that you have done all this work and just as you were beginning to feel good about the prospects of making a deal, you belatedly ask the seller if you can examine the leases. Here you discover a serious discrepancy. The seller has given you not what the tenants are actually paying but rather what they would be paying if he, soft-hearted philanthrope that he is, were charging as much as the other greedy capitalist roaders in the neighborhood. In other words, he lied. Now you know why he has no vacancies.

The real rent roll for 2014 looks like this:

10 studio apartments @ $650 each
30 1-bedroom apartments @ $850 each
8 2-bedroom apartments @ $1,000 each

Once you get done smashing your office furniture, you recognize that you need to start over and re-run all of your numbers. If you have been doing your work on a computer, go back to the file you called, "Original apartment case study."

For the first year, 2014, use the monthly rents shown directly above as the true rents. For the next four years, you can keep the amounts that you had in the original analysis. Why? Even though the seller wasn't actually charging the amounts he claimed for 2014, you agreed that those were indeed fair market rents for that year and that they would increase by 2% each subsequent year.

So, the fair market rent for the second year should be the amount you were originally planning on. It will be 2% more than the first-year's fair market rent, which is what the seller falsely claimed to be charging.

When the apartments were rented at below-market rates, the seller experienced no vacancy and you made no allowance other than 2% for uncollectable rent. What will happen when you impose significant rent increases? Some tenants will choose not to renew, and replacements will no longer be lined up three-deep in the hall. You need to adjust your thinking and provide a greater vacancy allowance in Year 2, followed by a moderate level in subsequent years. You decide on 6% for the second year and 4% thereafter.

Now revisit some of the questions you considered with the original case study. Most of your answers, of course will be different. Earlier I asked you to think like an investor and consider what kinds of returns might be acceptable. Do you feel that the same returns would be acceptable in this revised scenario as in the original? Why, or why not?

Revise your first-year rent figures, adjust the vacancy allowance for years two through five, and see how that $3 million asking price looks now.

	2014	2015	2016	2017	2018
GROSS INCOME	480,000	547,128	558,071	569,232	580,617
- Vacancy & Credit Allowance	9,600	32,828	22,323	22,769	23,225
- Operating Expenses	227,400	235,234	243,351	251,759	260,471
NET OPERATING INCOME	243,000	279,066	292,397	294,704	296,921
Capitalization Rate	8.10%	9.30%	9.75%	9.82%	9.90%
Debt Coverage Ratio	1.01	1.09	1.07	1.08	1.09

It's clear that you won't have anywhere near the 1.20 Debt Coverage Ratio you need to finance 70% of a $3 million purchase and your cap rate won't approach the 11% you believe prevails in this market.

The damage also extends beyond the first year. Even though you assume that the Gross Scheduled Rent for the second year and beyond will be the same as in your original projections, the Gross Operating Income and therefore your Net Operating Income for those years suffer due to your need for a substantial vacancy allowance. In the original version of this case study you accepted the seller's representation that the market rents had already been established. If you have to impose those market rents starting in the second year of your ownership (since the below-market rents are locked in for Year 1), then you must allow for the risk of vacancy while you try to accomplish this. You must also recognize your uncertainty about the true size of that risk. Is 6% enough, or will you lose even more as you try to get these apartments up to market rents?

Facing a much lower first-year NOI, you're certainly not going to pay $3 million and are no longer inclined to pay $2.54 or $2.6 million for the property. You decide to re-run your analysis at $2.2 million.

	2014	2015	2016	2017	2018
GROSS INCOME	480,000	547,128	558,071	569,232	580,617
- Vacancy & Credit Allowance	9,600	32,828	22,323	22,769	23,225
- Operating Expenses	227,400	235,234	243,351	251,759	260,471
NET OPERATING INCOME	243,000	279,066	292,397	294,704	296,921
Capitalization Rate	11.05%	12.68%	13.29%	13.40%	13.50%
Debt Coverage Ratio	1.29	1.39	1.37	1.38	1.39

At this reduced price, your first-year cap rate and Debt Coverage Ratio are both fine. Assuming your assumptions are sound about re-leasing the property at market rents, these two metrics continue to hold up well.

Now consider the resale and overall rates of return.

	2014	2015	2016	2017	2018
PROJECTED SELLING PRICE	2,209,000	2,537,000	2,658,000	2,679,000	2,699,000
- Costs of Sale	154,630	177,590	186,060	187,530	188,930
- 1st Mortgage Payoff	1,503,364	1,468,208	1,433,970	1,396,520	1,355,557
BEFORE-TAX SALE PROCEEDS	270,904	631,792	800,418	881,664	968,168
- Total Federal Tax on Sale	(7,462)	52,505	90,487	109,869	129,065
AFTER-TAX SALE PROCEEDS	278,366	579,287	709,931	771,795	839,103
IRR, Before Tax	-18.66%	40.17%	39.90%	35.53%	32.80%
Modified IRR, Before Tax	-18.66%	38.54%	36.83%	31.69%	28.40%
IRR, After-Tax	-20.06%	31.68%	32.10%	28.75%	26.67%
Modified IRR, After-Tax	-20.06%	30.70%	30.15%	26.27%	23.79%
PV, NOI & Reversion	2,069,703	2,360,365	2,466,675	2,494,552	2,519,157
PV, CFAT & Sale Proc. After Tax	288,646	576,281	694,497	750,524	811,266
EQUITY, excluding reserves	425,534	809,382	986,478	1,069,194	1,157,098
RETURN ON EQUITY (CFBT/equity)	12.95%	9.70%	8.04%	7.64%	7.25%

After the first year your return is substantial, but keep in mind that it is now based on the somewhat uncertain estimate of how much vacancy you'll incur getting this property up to speed. Being a prudent investor, you decide to see how the numbers look if your re-leasing assumptions are just a bit more apocalyptic. You re-run the analysis, this time estimating that in your first year of re-leasing (i.e. Year 2 of ownership), you'll lose 18% to vacancy and credit; in the following year you'll lose another 10%; and from that point on you'll level off at 4% as you maintain top rental rates.

	2014	2015	2016	2017	2018
PROJECTED SELLING PRICE	2,209,000	1,940,000	2,354,000	2,679,000	2,699,000
- Costs of Sale	154,630	135,800	164,780	187,530	188,930
- 1st Mortgage Payoff	1,503,364	1,468,208	1,433,970	1,396,520	1,355,557
- 2nd Mortgage Payoff	280,102	259,410	237,552	213,286	186,345
BEFORE-TAX SALE PROCEEDS	270,904	76,582	517,698	881,664	968,168
- Total Federal Tax on Sale	(7,462)	(7,051)	32,904	109,869	129,065
AFTER-TAX SALE PROCEEDS	278,366	83,633	484,794	771,795	839,103
IRR, Before Tax	-18.66%	-45.40%	17.80%	30.66%	28.62%
Modified IRR, Before Tax	-18.66%	-39.16%	16.91%	28.55%	26.14%
IRR, After-Tax	-20.06%	-45.85%	13.60%	24.96%	23.46%
Modified IRR, After-Tax	-20.06%	-40.95%	13.15%	23.61%	21.83%
PV, NOI & Reversion	2,069,703	1,856,457	2,182,182	2,416,782	2,441,386
PV, CFAT & Sale Proc. After Tax	288,646	85,385	469,047	750,524	811,266
EQUITY, excluding reserves	425,534	212,382	682,478	1,069,194	1,157,098
RETURN ON EQUITY (CFBT/equity)	12.95%	6.05%	6.72%	7.64%	7.25%

Not surprisingly, the high vacancy loss severely impacts the property's performance in the second year, despite the higher rental rates. The property begins to recover in the third year with another round of rent increases and a moderating vacancy rate. By the fourth year, the building has reached a stabilized rent and vacancy (or occupancy, since the glass is more than half full) and what appears to be an ample rate of return. Keep in mind that all of this is predicated now on a purchase price of $2.2 million, rather then the $3 million that your less-than-forthcoming seller was expecting.

Finally, let's consider a question that was raised before you began to re-run the numbers on this investment:

Do you feel that the same returns would be acceptable in this revised scenario as in the first?

To be sure, this is a matter of judgment – something that cannot be reduced to formulas and metrics. Still, a basic principle held by virtually all investors is that there must be a balance between risk and reward. You believed you were taking on less risk in the first scenario, when you presumed that market rents were already in place. In the second (and true) set of circumstances you face greater uncertainty as to the real cost involved in getting the property up to market.

You would surprise no one if you insisted on a higher return in the situation that presented the greater risk.

Let's review what you did and learned in this case study:

1. This was your first encounter with a standard, pre-existing income property, one that would be bought and sold strictly for its income stream. Its value was not a function of comparable sales data, i.e., the sales of other, similar properties, as was the case with the single-family. It was also not a development project, as you saw in the creation of an income property in the previous chapter.
2. You had an opportunity to work with a more complex set of factors, as you would in a real deal. You dealt with financing terms, closing costs, vacancy rates, etc., put them into a detailed pro forma, and then scrutinized them to understand why subsequent cash flows, sale proceeds, and rates of return behaved as they did.
3. You saw the importance of due diligence. It's easy to get so caught up in running numbers and evaluating projections that you forget to make sure your source data is genuine. The saying, "Garbage in, garbage out" is perfectly suited to income-property analysis. Failing to check and double-check the facts can be a costly mistake.
4. You had a chance to see the power of so-called "What if..?" analysis, particularly analysis driven by computer modeling. What happens if you lower the price; if you alter the loan terms; if you assume different rental rates; if you increase the vacancy allowance? Your goal is to make the best buying or selling decision possible. The ability to consider numerous variations on a theme greatly increases the likelihood that you can structure the deal for maximum benefit.
5. After you discovered a fundamental error in your basic assumptions about this property's income, you were able to take that "What if...?" power even further, quickly recasting the entire analysis to conform to the new, corrected information.

41

The Shopping Center

S
o far you've looked at a variety of residential and mixed-use properties. It's time now to turn your attention to something that's a bit different, a property that is strictly commercial: a small, strip shopping center.

Fundamentally, your analysis of this shopping center will be very much like what you did with the apartment building. An income property is essentially an income stream so you'll be concerned with the same cash flow, resale and rate-of-return issues. Like the apartment building, the shopping center's value will be a function of that income stream.

What's different about commercial property is the way the income stream is constructed. You typically rent space on a rate-per-square-foot basis. Leases tend to be longer, often with built-in increases and options to renew. Tenants may reimburse you for some portion of your operating expenses. And your depreciation allowance is less generous.

The Facts

A. The Property

The Space Center is a 10,000 square-foot strip shopping center located in Soleado, Florida. The building is 20 years old. It is in good condition and still has its original flat roof. The property is not located in a flood plain. Annual property taxes are currently $16,702, an increase of 2% over the previous year. The tax assessment on the current Grand List is $584,000, of which $432,160 is for the building and $151,840 is the land. It has paved parking for 18 cars. Each unit has its own electric, gas and water meters. There are also house meters for electricity (outside lighting) and for water (for one spigot to water plantings). Mechanicals are maintained by the tenants and are all in good condition.

B. The Location

The road on which this property is located is one of three principal thorough-fares in the town. The area is stable and there has been some new commercial construction over the past several years. The road is fairly well built up, although there are some stretches of vacant land. Properties are mostly small commercial (strip centers, fast food, automotive, local family-style restaurants, small office buildings) with light industrial mixed in. Unemployment is low in Soleado and the median family income is slightly above the national average. School-age population has grown faster than expected; a new elementary school is planned to open in September of 2015 and an addition to the high school will be needed by September of 2016. It never snows in sunny Soleado.

C. The Tenants

1. Belinda's Trips (travel agency) - 1,400 sf - She pays $12.50 per square foot per year plus a pro-rata share of property taxes over the base amount of $10,000 (i.e., the property owner pays the first $10,000 of property taxes for the entire center and Belinda pays a share of the rest based on her unit's square footage compared to the total square footage of the center). Her current lease term expires June 30, 2015. She has an option for an additional five years at $15/sf/yr. She has been here for 3½ years and has done well. You are going to assume that she'll exercise her option for an additional five years. However, you will hedge your bet about what will happen after that. You estimate that you can find a new tenant at that time at $17.50/sf but also that you'll have a "rollover vacancy" – a vacancy in a particular unit resulting from a rollover to a new tenant. In a perfect world a new tenant would move in and start paying rent just as the previous tenant departs, but you expect to lose three

months' rent (at the previous rate) as well as three months of expense recoveries.

2. Y1.8K (antiques dealer) - 1,600 sf - This tenant pays $12.50 per square foot per year plus the same pro rata share of taxes over the base. His rent has scheduled increases to $13.50/sf on 8/1/2017, and $15.50 on 8/1/2021. The lease expires 7/31/2025. He has been in the center for about two years. He started off slowly, but has been doing much better.

3. Vacant space - 1,400 sf – The previous tenant went out of business and left without notice three months ago. You've found a new tenant – Wiggley's Sushi Bar and Live Bait Shop. They will take occupancy on 3/1/2014 but will not start paying rent until 5/1/2014. You must also pay a leasing commission of $4,284 on 5/1/2014. You're going to give a "tenant improvement allowance" of $3,000 so the tenant can upgrade the electric service to accommodate their coolers. The lease is for an initial term of five years starting at $14.50/sf plus property tax pass-through. There is a bump to $16.50 per sf on 5/1/2017. There is also an option to renew on 5/1/2019 for five more years starting at $18.00 for the first two years of the renewal, and $19.00 for the last three years.

4. The Contraltos Family Pest Control and Extermination – 1,600 sf – The tenant pays $11.00/sf plus the same pro rata property tax pass-through as other tenants. The lease runs through 2/2018 with no escalations. The good news: they are certain to renew for another 10 years at end of the lease. The bad news: they are uncommonly persuasive negotiators.

5. Out, Damned Spot! (dry cleaner) – 1,400 sf – The tenant pays $13.50/sf/yr plus the same pro rata share of taxes over base. Her rent is scheduled to increase to $15.50/sf on 6/1/2017. She has an option for $18.50 on 6/1/2022. She has been here for a very long time, so you are confident she will renew.

6. Tortist and O'Hare (walk-in legal clinic) – 1,200 sf, paying $14/sf/yr – They also pay a pro-rata share of taxes over the same base. Their lease calls for a $0.25 per square foot increase

on March 1 every year through 2018. You are uncertain regarding their likelihood to renew in 2019, but estimate a market rate of $16.50 per sf in that year. Once again you are going to be conservative and assume a rollover vacancy of three months.

7. Cut & Run (hair salon) – 1,400 sf, $13.50/sf/yr – She has the same deal with property taxes. The lease runs at the current rate through November, 2018, and then escalates to $16.50 through November 2023. She is a long-time tenant and you expect she'll stay.

D. Operating Expenses, 2013

Accounting	1,800
Advertising	1,500
Insurance (fire and liability)	6,250
Legal	2,150
Miscellaneous	1,875
Property Management, 3% of gross operating income	
Repairs and Maintenance	5,475
Supplies	1,400
Taxes, Real Estate	16,702
Trash Removal	3,600
Utilities – Electricity, outside lighting	1,175
Utilities – Sewer and Water	775
Utilities – Telephone	350

You estimate that expenses other than property management will be 2% higher in the year 2014, the first year of your analysis. Thereafter, they will increase by no less than 2% annually, but some items may increase faster. Make what you feel are reasonable projections.

E. Financing

Financing is available in this market at 65% loan-to-value. Rates are currently 8.0%, 20-year term with two points payable at closing. The interest rate may adjust annually; the maximum increase is 1% per year. You believe that rates will rise, but not above 11.5%.

F. Taxation

For purposes of this analysis you will assume the investor is an individual tax-payer with a marginal tax bracket of 28% and an Adjusted Gross Income in excess of $150,000.

G. Other Considerations

Commercial income properties in this area have been selling at a capitalization rate of 10.5%. Net Operating Income for the property last year was $80,325. A reasonable Vacancy and Credit Loss allowance for this property would be a nominal amount. Remember that you have already imposed a rollover vacancy for each of the two units you think may require re-renting during the span of your analysis, 2014 – 2023. Those specific rollover vacancies reduced the property's projected income, so you don't need to account for them again.

The current market rent for space in a strip center such as this is about $15 per square foot per year. You believe the market will rise, on average, about 2% per year.

The Problem

This case study takes you another step closer to a real world situation. It provides you with a lot of hard facts, but unlike the previous examples it doesn't try to provide every number you need to work with. In some areas, you have just anecdotal information rather than actual numbers. You're going to have to make judgments of your own as to what implications, if any, that information will have on your projections for this property. In this example, as in life generally, there's a shortage of perfect information and of unarguably correct answers.

Base your analysis of this property on a 10-year holding period ending in 2023. The presentation should represent what you believe to be the most likely stream of income over that time.

As you build your projections, consider the following issues:

1. Based on the income stream, what do you believe is the buyer's estimate of the market value of the property at the time of acquisition?
2. Are there any factors concerning the physical property that could adversely affect its future cash flow? If so, how might you deal with them?
3. Given the information at your disposal, what do you believe are reasonable estimates of the property's value over the next 10 years?

The Analysis

The key difference between a commercial property like this and a residential property such as you saw in the last chapter is in the way you will account for and forecast its income. In general you treat apartments as units, each generating a specific amount of rent. Most commercial real estate is rented instead by the square foot. You typically have longer leases with commercial property, so in one regard the income stream is more predictable. However, it can be more difficult and time-consuming to find a suitable tenant for commercial space than it does for residential, so you often need to allow for spikes of vacancy when leases come up for renewal.

In order to secure a commercial tenant, it may be necessary for you to make some initial financial concessions or abatements, or to provide an allowance for improvements to the tenant's space. On the other hand, it is quite common for the tenant to pay a pro rata share of some of your operating expenses, something you seldom see with apartment rentals.

In this case study you'll encounter most of these commercial property characteristics. In order to make both the calculations and presentations as straightforward as possible, I've used the Standard Edition of RealData's *Real Estate Investment Analysis* software to work through this case study. For clarity, I have occasionally edited the output to remove some items normally displayed by the software but not relevant to the case at hand.

Your approach to the income portion of the analysis will be a bit different from what it was with the residential property. It was easy to group similar residential units together, such as 10 studio apartments at $700 each. Since commercial property rents by the square foot and the leases may contain a variety of interim escalations and options to renew, it is usually necessary to sort out the income on a unit by unit basis.

On the following seven pages you'll see summaries of what you might expect the income to be from each of the seven spaces in this shopping center. Let's look at some of these in detail now.

The first space is home to Belinda's Trips. She occupies 1,400 square feet at a rent that is currently $12.50 per square foot per year. Her base rent, therefore is $17,500 per year. Since the center has a total of 10,000 rentable square feet, she occupies 14% and so her pro-rata share of recoverable expenses is 14%. If you go back to the original facts, you'll see that the tenants must each pay a pro-rata share of property taxes in excess of $10,000. This amount (the $10,000) is called a base or an "expense stop" because it is the point at which the landlord stops paying the expense and passes the rest on to the tenants.

For the moment, please take on faith that the correct total amount for property taxes in 2014 is $17,036. The tenants as a group are responsible for $7,036, which is the amount in excess of $10,000. Belinda's share is 14% of $7,036, or $985.

Commercial leases generally characterize recoverable expenses, or "pass-throughs" as they are often called, as additional rent. That's because the tenant doesn't really pay the expense directly. Would you rely on a third party to pay your taxes or insurance on time? Rather, the landlord pays the expense, the tenant reimburses the landlord, and the amount is classified as additional rent. Hence Belinda's total rent for 2014 is $18,485.

UNIT: 1	Tenant: Belinda's Trips then rollover	2014 Initial Rate: 12.50 $/sf/year					Rentable SF: 1,400		
	2014	2015	2016	2017	2018	2019	2020	2021	2022	2023
Rent Change Schedule										
Month of Change (1 - 12)	0	7	0	0	0	0	10	0	0	0
% Change, or New Rate	0.0000	15.0000	0.0000	0.0000	0.0000	0.0000	17.5000	0.0000	0.0000	0.0000
Unit of measure	% change	$/sf/year % change	% change	% change	% change	% change	$/sf/year % change	$/sf/year % change	$/sf/year % change	% change
Total Base Rent, $ (calculated)	17,500	19,250	21,000	21,000	21,000	21,000	21,875	24,500	24,500	24,500
Expense recoveries, based on 14.00% of total	985	1,080	1,254	1,334	1,416	1,500	1,587	1,677	1,769	1,864
Other Rental Revenue	0	0	0	0	0	0	0	0	0	0
Concessions, Abatements and Rollover Vacancy Loss	(0)	(0)	(0)	(0)	(0)	(0)	(5,647)	(0)	(0)	(0)
Tenant Improvements, $ or $/sf (if 500 or less)	0	0	0	0	0	0	0	0	0	0
Month placed in service	0	0	0	0	0	0	0	0	0	0
Commissions paid	0	0	0	0	0	0	0	0	0	0
Month paid (1 - 12)	0	0	0	0	0	0	0	0	0	0
Number of months to capitalize commission	0	0	0	0	0	0	0	0	0	0
TOTAL UNIT INCOME - 1:	18,485	20,330	22,254	22,334	22,416	22,500	17,815	26,177	26,269	26,364

UNIT: 2	Tenant: Y1.8K		2014 Initial Rate: 12.50 $/sf/year					Rentable SF: 1,600		
	2014	2015	2016	2017	2018	2019	2020	2021	2022	2023
Rent Change Schedule										
Month of Change (1 - 12)	0	0	0	8	0	0	0	8	0	0
% Change, or New Rate	0.0000	0.0000	0.0000	13.5000	0.0000	0.0000	0.0000	15.5000	0.0000	0.0000
Unit of measure	% change	% change	% change	$/sf/year	% change	% change	% change	$/sf/year	% change	% change
Total Base Rent, $ (calculated)	20,000	20,000	20,000	20,667	21,600	21,600	21,600	22,933	24,800	24,800
Expense recoveries, based on 16.00% of total	1,126	1,235	1,433	1,524	1,618	1,714	1,814	1,916	2,022	2,130
Other Rental Revenue	0	0	0	0	0	0	0	0	0	0
Concessions, Abatements and Rollover Vacancy Loss	(0)	(0)	(0)	(0)	(0)	(0)	(0)	(0)	(0)	(0)
Tenant Improvements, $ or $/sf (if 500 or less)	0	0	0	0	0	0	0	0	0	0
Month placed in service	0	0	0	0	0	0	0	0	0	0
Commissions paid	0	0	0	0	0	0	0	0	0	0
Month paid (1 - 12)	0	0	0	0	0	0	0	0	0	0
Number of months to capitalize commission	0	0	0	0	0	0	0	0	0	0
TOTAL UNIT INCOME - 2:	21,126	21,235	21,433	22,191	23,218	23,314	23,414	24,850	26,822	26,930

UNIT:	3	Tenant:	Vacant, then Wiggley's 2014 Initial Rate:	0.00	$/sf/year		Rentable SF:	1,400	
	2014	**2015**	**2016**	**2017**	**2018**	**2019**	**2020**	**2021**	**2022**	**2023**
Rent Change Schedule										
Month of Change (1 - 12)	5	0	0	5	0	5	0	5	0	0
% Change, or New Rate	14.5000	0.0000	0.0000	16.5000	0.0000	18.0000	0.0000	19.0000	0.0000	0.0000
Unit of measure	$/sf/year	% change	% change	$/sf/year	% change	$/sf/year	% change	$/sf/year	% change	% change
Total Base Rent, $ (calculated)	13,533	20,300	20,300	22,167	23,100	24,500	25,200	26,133	26,600	26,600
Expense recoveries, based on 14.00% of total	657	1,080	1,254	1,334	1,416	1,500	1,587	1,677	1,769	1,864
Other Rental Revenue	0	0	0	0	0	0	0	0	0	0
Concessions, Abatements and Rollover Vacancy Loss	(0)	(0)	(0)	(0)	(0)	(0)	(0)	(0)	(0)	(0)
Tenant Improvements, $ or $/sf (if 500 or less)	3,000	0	0	0	0	0	0	0	0	0
Month placed in service	5	0	0	0	0	0	0	0	0	0
Commissions paid	4,284	0	0	0	0	0	0	0	0	0
Month paid (1 - 12)	5	0	0	0	0	0	0	0	0	0
Number of months to capitalize commission	60	0	0	0	0	0	0	0	0	0
TOTAL UNIT INCOME - 3:	14,190	21,380	21,554	23,500	24,516	26,000	26,787	27,810	28,369	28,464

UNIT:	4	Tenant:	The Contraltos		2014 Initial Rate:	11.00	$/sf/year		Rentable SF:	1,600
	2014	2015	2016	2017	2018	2019	2020	2021	2022	2023
Rent Change Schedule										
Month of Change (1 - 12)	0	0	0	0	3	0	0	0	0	3
% Change, or New Rate	0.0000	0.0000	0.0000	0.0000	14.0000	0.0000	0.0000	0.0000	0.0000	17.0000
Unit of measure	% change	% change	% change	% change	$/sf/year	% change	% change	% change	% change	$/sf/year
Total Base Rent, $ (calculated)	17,600	17,600	17,600	17,600	21,600	22,400	22,400	22,400	22,400	26,400
Expense recoveries, based on 16.00% of total	1,126	1,235	1,433	1,524	1,618	1,714	1,814	1,916	2,022	2,130
Other Rental Revenue	0	0	0	0	0	0	0	0	0	0
Concessions, Abatements and Rollover Vacancy Loss	(0)	(0)	(0)	(0)	(0)	(0)	(0)	(0)	(0)	(0)
Tenant Improvements, $ or $/sf (if 500 or less)	0	0	0	0	0	0	0	0	0	0
Month placed in service	0	0	0	0	0	0	0	0	0	0
Commissions paid	0	0	0	0	0	0	0	0	0	0
Month paid (1 - 12)	0	0	0	0	0	0	0	0	0	0
Number of months to capitalize commission	0	0	0	0	0	0	0	0	0	0
TOTAL UNIT INCOME - 4:	18,726	18,835	19,033	19,124	23,218	24,114	24,214	24,316	24,422	28,530

UNIT:	5	Tenant:	Out, Damned Spot!	2014 Initial Rate:	13.50	$/sf/year	Rentable SF:	1,400	
		2014	**2015**	**2016**	**2017**	**2018**	**2019**	**2020**	**2021**	**2022**	**2023**
Rent Change Schedule											
Month of Change (1 - 12)		0	0	0	6	0	0	0	0	6	0
% Change, or New Rate		0.0000	0.0000	0.0000	15.5000	0.0000	0.0000	0.0000	0.0000	18.5000	0.0000
Unit of measure		% change	% change	% change	$/sf/year	% change	% change	% change	% change	$/sf/year	% change
Total Base Rent, $ (calculated)		18,900	18,900	18,900	20,533	21,700	21,700	21,700	21,700	24,150	25,900
Expense recoveries, based on 14.00% of total		985	1,080	1,254	1,334	1,416	1,500	1,587	1,677	1,769	1,864
Other Rental Revenue		0	0	0	0	0	0	0	0	0	0
Concessions, Abatements and Rollover Vacancy Loss		(0)	(0)	(0)	(0)	(0)	(0)	(0)	(0)	(0)	(0)
Tenant Improvements, $ or $/sf (if 500 or less)		0	0	0	0	0	0	0	0	0	0
Month placed in service		0	0	0	0	0	0	0	0	0	0
Commissions paid		0	0	0	0	0	0	0	0	0	0
Month paid (1 - 12)		0	0	0	0	0	0	0	0	0	0
Number of months to capitalize commission		0	0	0	0	0	0	0	0	0	0
TOTAL UNIT INCOME - 5:		19,885	19,980	20,154	21,867	23,116	23,200	23,287	23,377	25,919	27,764

UNIT: 6	Tenant: Tortist & O'Hare then rollover	2014 Initial Rate:	14.00 $/sf/year		Rentable SF:	1,200			
	2014	2015	2016	2017	2018	2019	2020	2021	2022	2023
Rent Change Schedule										
Month of Change (1 - 12)	3	3	3	3	3	6	0	0	0	0
% Change, or New Rate	14.2500	14.5000	14.7500	15.0000	15.2500	16.5000	0.0000	0.0000	0.0000	0.0000
Unit of measure	$/sf/year	$/sf/year	$/sf/year	$/sf/year	$/sf/year	$/sf/year	% change	% change	% change	% change
Total Base Rent, $ (calculated)	17,050	17,350	17,650	17,950	18,250	19,175	19,800	19,800	19,800	19,800
Expense recoveries, based on 12.00% of total	844	926	1,075	1,143	1,213	1,286	1,360	1,437	1,516	1,598
Other Rental Revenue	0	0	0	0	0	0	0	0	0	0
Concessions, Abatements and Rollover Vacancy Loss	(0)	(0)	(0)	(0)	(0)	(4,896)	(0)	(0)	(0)	(0)
Tenant Improvements, $ or $/sf (if 500 or less)	0	0	0	0	0	0	0	0	0	0
Month placed in service	0	0	0	0	0	0	0	0	0	0
Commissions paid	0	0	0	0	0	0	0	0	0	0
Month paid (1 - 12)	0	0	0	0	0	0	0	0	0	0
Number of months to capitalize commission	0	0	0	0	0	0	0	0	0	0
TOTAL UNIT INCOME - 6:	17,894	18,276	18,725	19,093	19,463	15,564	21,160	21,237	21,316	21,398

UNIT: 7	Tenant: Cut & Run				2014 Initial Rate: 13.50 $/sf/year			Rentable SF: 1,400	
	2014	2015	2016	2017	2018	2019	2020	2021	2022	2023
Rent Change Schedule										
Month of Change (1 - 12)	0	0	0	0	12	0	0	0	0	12
% Change, or New Rate	0.0000	0.0000	0.0000	0.0000	16.5000	0.0000	0.0000	0.0000	0.0000	19.0000
Unit of measure	% change	% change	% change	% change	$/sf/year	% change	% change	% change	% change	$/sf/year
Total Base Rent, $ (calculated)	18,900	18,900	18,900	18,900	19,250	23,100	23,100	23,100	23,100	23,392
Expense recoveries, based on 14.00% of total	985	1,080	1,254	1,334	1,416	1,500	1,587	1,677	1,769	1,864
Other Rental Revenue	0	0	0	0	0	0	0	0	0	0
Concessions, Abatements and Rollover Vacancy Loss	(0)	(0)	(0)	(0)	(0)	(0)	(0)	(0)	(0)	(0)
Tenant Improvements, $ or $/sf (if 500 or less)	0	0	0	0	0	0	0	0	0	0
Month placed in service	0	0	0	0	0	0	0	0	0	0
Commissions paid										
Month paid (1 - 12)	0	0	0	0	0	0	0	0	0	0
Number of months to capitalize commission	0	0	0	0	0	0	0	0	0	0
TOTAL UNIT INCOME - 7:	19,885	19,980	20,154	20,234	20,666	24,600	24,687	24,777	24,869	25,256

Belinda's base rent (i.e., the amount before pass-throughs) increases to $15 per square foot in the middle of 2015, so the total base rent for that year ($19,250) is a blend of six months at the old rate of $12.50 and six at $15. Notice that the expense recovery for real estate taxes rises in 2015, and for that matter in every year. Why? Because when you get to your APOD you'll be making the rash assumption that property taxes will go up every year.

For 2016 through 2019, Belinda pays a full year at $15 per square foot, or $21,000 plus expense recoveries. At the end of June, 2020 her lease expires and you've decided to assume that you'll have to deal with a rollover at that time. You estimate that the space will sit empty for three months, or at least generate no income while a new tenant gets it ready to open for business. After those three months you expect to begin collecting $17.50 per square foot.

Let's break down the year 2020 to see how you compute the total income for that unit. Your rent at the beginning of the year is $15 per square foot, and you expect it to rise to $17.50 starting with the tenth month. If there were no rollover vacancy to consider, you would have nine months at $15 and three months at $17.50. Do the math:

1,400 sf x 15/sf = 21,000 per year / 12 = 1,750 per month

1,400 sf x 17.50/sf = 24,500 per year / 12 = 2,041.67 per month

(1,750 x 9 months) + (2,041.67 x 3 months) = 21,875

With no rollover vacancy, you would receive $21,875 in base rent. However, with this space generating no income for the three months before your new $17.50 rent kicks in, you lose 3 x $1,750, or $5,250.

What about expense recoveries? Again, since you haven't seen the APOD yet, accept on faith that the total estimated property taxes for 2020 are $21,337. (If ye are of little faith, take the 2013 tax amount of $16,702 given in the case study facts above, and increase it as follow: 2% for 2014, 4% for 2015, 7% for 2016, and 3% thereafter.)

Tenants pay their share of taxes in excess of the $10,000 base, so this unit should absorb 14% of $11,337 for the year. That equals $1,587 per year, or $132.25 per month. Since there will be no tenant in the space for three months, you expect to lose 3 x $132.25 or $397 in expense recoveries. Your total rollover vacancy costs you the $5,250 you lose in base rent plus the $397 in expenses you could not recover, or $5,647. That leaves you with expected income of $17,815 from this unit in rollover year 2020.

With Unit 2, the antiques store Y1.8K, you're looking at periodic increases in the base rent at dates and in amounts specified in the lease. The increases in rent occur in August of 2017 and 2021, so as with Unit 1 you need to blend two different rental rates in those years. If you haven't done so already, make those calculations and compare your results against the base rents shown above for Unit 2.

Since Y1.8K's lease doesn't expire until 2025 and your analysis goes only to 2023, you have no rollover issues to deal with here, but as with all the tenants in this center, you have the expense recovery as additional income for this unit.

Unit 3 presents several new issues for you to grapple with. The first is that the space is vacant when your analysis begins on January 1, 2014. How do you deal with that? The simplest way is to recognize that, although you have 1,400 square of rentable space sitting there, you have an initial rate of $0. Not what you would prefer, but it is what it is.

Happily, you have a tenant ready to move in. As is fairly common with commercial space, especially retail, this tenant will take occupancy on a given date but the rent clock won't start running for a few months. The tenant wants time to fit up the space. Chain stores especially may have a signature layout and décor that they need to construct before they open to the public. During that time they are not doing business. They typically expect to have access to the space for some period of time rent free, so they can build it out.

Wiggley's Sushi Bar and Live Bait Shop may not exactly be a powerhouse franchise, but you're glad to get someone into this space. So, while their lease begins in March and they are able to enter and work on the space then, their rent cycle doesn't begin until May.

There are some other costs you incur as you get this tenancy set up. Mr. Wiggley has asked you for what is called a tenant improvement. That doesn't mean he wants you to find someone better to replace him. Rather, he wants you to pay for an improvement to his space. In this case, he needs to upgrade the electric service so he can run the coolers required to keep his sushi fresh. You contemplate the alternative and decide that the $3,000 he asked for is well worth it.

You would like to think of this as an operating expense, but later in the analysis you'll find that the software you're using has properly recognized it as a capital cost and depreciated it accordingly. A capital cost is one that you typically cannot write off in a single year, as you can with an operating expense. There are a number of such costs that you'll encounter as a real estate investor. A capital improvement, whether to the property as a whole or for the benefit of a single tenant, is certainly one such cost.

There are other costs that also must be "amortized" over some number of years, such as leasing commissions, loan points, and closing costs to acquire an investment property. The number of years over which you deduct these costs varies according to the circumstances. For example, the points on a 20-year investment loan would normally be written off over 20 years, but if that loan requires a five-year balloon payment (see Chapter 29), then you would amortize them over five years.

You required the services of a leasing agent to find Mr. Wiggley and must pay her a commission of $4,284 for the first five-year term of the lease. That commission is due in May, as soon as you receive your first rent check. Notice that the software shown above asks you to specify the number of months over which to capitalize (i.e., amortize) the commission, and you've entered "60." As discussed previously, you generally must capitalize a commission over the term of the lease, so this cost will be written off over 60 months starting in May, 2014.

Let's take a look at your analysis of the first year for Unit 3. Your starting rent is $0, and it changes to $14.50 per square foot in the fifth month.

1,400 sf x 14.50/sf = 20,300 per year / 12 = 1,691.67 per month

1,691.67 x 8 months = 13,533 base rent

In regard to recoverable expenses, Wiggley's occupies 14% of the total space, as does Belinda, in Unit 1. Like Belinda, he would be obligated to pay 14% of $7,036, or $985 if he were on the hook for all of 2014 – but he's not. Wiggley's is only responsible to pay for the eight months from May to the end of the year.

If $985 is the full annual amount, then

985 / 12 = 82.08

is the monthly amount, and

8 x 82.08 = 657

is the amount he owes for eight months.

You expect to receive $13,533 in base rent and $657 in expense recoveries in 2014, for a total unit income of $14,190 – while keeping in mind that you'll also be out-of-pocket $3,000 for improvements and $4,284 in commission costs.

Matters get a good deal simpler in the second and third years. You have a full year of rent and expense recoveries coming in during each of 2015 and 2016. In May, 2017, the rent rises to $16.50 per square foot, making for yet another of those blended rent calculations at which you've now become so proficient: 1,400 square feet, four months at $14.50 plus eight months at $16.50 equals $22,167.

Wiggley's has an option to renew in 2019. Somehow this store just reeks of success and so you're confident that he will stay. Hence your analysis shows an increase to $18 per square foot in the option year and to $19 per square foot in 2021, at the start of the renewed lease.

By the time you reach Unit 4, The Contraltos Family Pest Control and Extermination, the math has become routine. The only issue here is to make a judgment about the rental rate for their new lease in 2018. The tenant summary above didn't specify a rate; it merely said, "The good news: they are certain to renew for another 10 years at end of the lease. The bad news: they are uncommonly persuasive negotiators." You decide on $14 per square foot in 2018 and $17 in 2023.

With Unit 5 – Out, Damned Spot! Dry Cleaners – you're back to a straightforward analysis. A rent increase to $15.50 is scheduled for 2017, and she has a renewal option for $18.50 in 2022 that you are confident she will exercise.

Unit 6 is a bit more problematic. It is occupied by a walk-in legal clinic whose lease calls for an annual increase of $0.25 per square foot. You doubt that they will renew when their lease expires in 2019. You estimate that you can re-rent the space then for $16.50 per square foot, but also assume that you'll have a rollover vacancy of three months.

If you look at the income summary for Unit 6, above, you'll see that the rent per square foot increases $0.25 each year in month 3 until 2019, when it changes instead to $16.50 per square foot in month 6. You've assumed a loss of three months' rent and expense recoveries due to the rollover, as you did in the similar situation with Unit 1. Let's see again how you calculate that loss.

The tenant's fifth and final rent increase is to $15.25 per square foot, so that is the rate that is in place when they leave. 1,200 square feet at $15.25 per square foot equals an annual rent of $18,300, or $1,525 per month. With this space producing no rent for the three months before you begin to collect your new $16.50 rate, you lose 3 x $1,525, or $4,575.

As you can see in the report, your expense recoveries for the full year should have been $1,286, or $107.17 per month. You lose three months of these as well, or $321. Your total rollover loss, then, is $4,575 in base rent plus $321 in expense recoveries, or $4,896.

The rollover takes a bite out of your income for 2019, dropping the total you take in from this unit to $15,564, down from $19,463 the previous year.

You might call your final lessee, the hair salon Cut & Run, a permanent sort of tenant. Her lease is locked in through November of 2023. She has an escalation built into the lease in December of 2018, so her total rent for that year represents 11 months at her previous rent of $13.50 and one month at the new rate of $16.50. Because she's a long-time tenant you expect her to renew in 2023, especially if you offer what you think is a conservative rent at that time, $19 per square foot. Even if you're wrong about her renewing, that misjudgment won't have much of an impact on your projections because it would affect only the last month of the last year of your analysis.

Once you aggregate all this information, your annual gross income should look like this:

2014	2015	2016	2017	2018
130,191	140,017	143,308	148,343	156,612

2019	2020	2021	2022	2023
159,294	161,365	172,544	177,986	184,707

You've worked your way through your income projections for this commercial property on a unit-by-unit basis, dealing with a lot of issues that are specific to this kind of property – issues such as expense recoveries, escalations, rollover vacancy and tenant improvements. The remainder of your analysis will be very much like that for any income property, residential or commercial, where you'll focus on operating expenses, cash flows, resale, and rates of return.

So, now it's time to build your Annual Property Operating Data form. You've already accounted for the potential vacancy loss due to tenant rollovers so, as the "Facts" section above suggests, you can choose a nominal allowance to account for potential credit loss or possibly an additional vacancy. Let's allow 2% each year.

Next you need to project your operating expenses. Remember that you were given the 2013 amounts for each expense, along with the advice that those expenses would be 2% higher in the 2014, the first year of the analysis. According to the information provided, expenses will increase by no less than 2% annually but a few items may increase faster, so you need to make some judgments.

Start by increasing the 2013 figures each by 2% to get your expenses for 2014, the start of your projections. Keep in mind that the property management expense is slated to be an estimate equal to 3% of each year's Gross Operating Income.

	2013	2014
Accounting	1,800	1,836
Advertising	1,500	1,530
Insurance (fire and liab.)	6,250	6,375
Legal	2,150	2,193
Miscellaneous	1,875	1,913
Property Management, 3% Gross Operating Income		3,828
Repairs and Maintenance	5,475	5,585
Supplies	1,400	1,428
Taxes, Real Estate	16,702	17,036
Trash Removal	3,600	3,672
Utilities Electricity	1,175	1,199
Utilities Sewer and Water	775	791
Utilities Telephone	350	357

Note that to calculate the management expense for 2014 you start with income for that year of $130,191 (as shown earlier where you totaled the income from all units). You then subtract 2% for vacancy and credit allowance, leaving a Gross

Operating Income of $127,587. Your property management expense is 3% of that figure, or $3,828.

You have enough information to build a one-year projection of expenses, but you want to extend your forecast out 10 years as you did with your unit-by-unit income summary. You were told to assume that expenses would increase by at least 2% each year, but that certain expenses might grow faster. It's time for you to make more judgments Your experience has been that services and utilities grow in cost as least as rapidly as inflation, so you're going to estimate those at 3%. Every year you're incredulous when you see your bill for insurance coverage, so you estimate that to rise at 6%. You believe in keeping your property well-maintained, so you let your estimate for that cost grow by 5% per year.

Finally, there is the question of property taxes. In the description of this community that you read in the "Facts" section, you noticed that the town is opening a new elementary school in 2015 and a new high school in 2016. It doesn't take a great deal of imagination to guess what those new facilities will do to your property tax bill. You decide to estimate a 4% increase for 2015, a 7% increase for 2016 and 3% for each year thereafter. You hope that will be enough, and decide to keep in the back of your mind that even greater tax increases might be necessary for the ongoing operation of those schools.

You now have enough information to construct that APOD and extend it from 2014 to 2023. Start with the expenses for 2014 as shown on the previous page. Keep property management at 3% of the GOI each year and increase most of the other expenses by 2% per year. Increase insurance, maintenance, property taxes, electricity and sewer and water as discussed above. You should end up with numbers like those shown on the next page.

You notice that you have a meaningful increase in Net Operating Income in the second year. Why? Remember that you started off the first year with a vacant unit that didn't begin producing rent until May. In the second year you received a full 12 months of rent from that space as well as a rent increase from Belinda's Trips. As you look through the NOI projections for all 10 years, your income seems to spike in 2018 and 2021. Again, if you go back to your projections for the individual units, you'll find that you projected renewals at higher rents for two or three units in each of those years.

	2014	2015	2016	2017	2018	2019	2020	2021	2022	2023
TOTAL GROSS INCOME	130,191	140,017	143,308	148,343	156,612	159,294	161,365	172,544	177,986	184,707
VACANCY & CREDIT ALLOWANCE	2,604	2,800	2,866	2,967	3,132	3,186	3,227	3,451	3,560	3,694
GROSS OPERATING INCOME	127,587	137,217	140,442	145,376	153,480	156,108	158,138	169,093	174,427	181,013
OPERATING EXPENSES										
Accounting	1,836	1,873	1,910	1,948	1,987	2,027	2,068	2,109	2,151	2,194
Advertising	1,530	1,561	1,592	1,624	1,656	1,689	1,723	1,757	1,793	1,828
Insurance (fire and liability)	6,375	6,758	7,163	7,593	8,048	8,531	9,043	9,586	10,161	10,770
Legal	2,193	2,237	2,282	2,327	2,374	2,421	2,470	2,519	2,569	2,621
Miscellaneous	1,913	1,951	1,990	2,030	2,071	2,112	2,154	2,197	2,241	2,286
Property Management	3,828	4,117	4,213	4,361	4,604	4,683	4,744	5,073	5,233	5,430
Repairs and Maintenance	5,585	5,864	6,157	6,465	6,789	7,128	7,484	7,859	8,252	8,664
Supplies	1,428	1,457	1,486	1,515	1,546	1,577	1,608	1,640	1,673	1,707
Taxes - Real Estate	17,036	17,717	18,958	19,526	20,112	20,716	21,337	21,977	22,636	23,316
Trash Removal	3,672	3,782	3,896	4,012	4,133	4,257	4,385	4,516	4,652	4,791
Utilities - Electricity	1,199	1,235	1,272	1,310	1,349	1,390	1,432	1,475	1,519	1,564
Utilities - Sewer and Water	791	815	839	864	890	917	944	973	1,002	1,032
Utilities - Telephone	357	364	371	379	386	394	402	410	418	427
TOTAL OPERATING EXPENSES	47,743	49,730	52,129	53,956	55,946	57,842	59,794	62,091	64,300	66,631
NET OPERATING INCOME	79,845	87,487	88,312	91,420	97,534	98,266	98,344	107,002	110,127	114,382

It's time for you to move on to projections of cash flow, resale and rates of return. Although this is a commercial property, your analysis from this point on will differ very little from what you did with the apartment building in the previous chapter. Remember, analyzing an income property investment means forecasting and analyzing its income stream. You've done the heavy lifting in your commercial lease analysis and are now close to having fully defined that income stream.

Close, but not quite there. You still have a few issues to sort out and a few more judgments to make.

1. Of course, in order to make any projections you need to presume a particular purchase price. The problem didn't specify a price, but it did say that the prevailing cap rate for properties like this in your market is 10.5% and that the NOI for the last full year of the current owner's operation, 2013, was $80,325. By now, the formula from Chapter 10 should be burned into your consciousness and you can use it to derive an estimate of value:

    Value = Net Operating Income / Capitalization Rate

    Value = 80,325 / .105

    Value = 765,000

2. One of the questions posed above should be hovering in the back of your mind: *"Are there any factors concerning the physical property that could adversely affect its future cash flow? If so, how might you deal with them?"* Raise your hand if you said this building is 20 years old and still has its original flat roof. There's no point in kidding yourself. It's not a question of if you'll need to replace the roof, but when. Twenty-five years is an optimistic life expectancy for a flat roof, so you had better plan to do this work by 2018. The case study didn't tell you how much a roof will cost, so you make an executive decision to estimate $40,000.

3. In the previous examples, your deduction for depreciation was fairly straightforward. In this situation, however, there are a few extra wrinkles. First of all, the useful life for non-residential property is longer than that for residential: 39 years as of this writing. Second, you need to

estimate the amount of depreciation allowed each year not only for the building, but also for the tenant improvement and for the new roof.

Remember that only the building and other improvements are depreciable, not the land. You know that the building is assessed at $432,160 and the land at $151,840 for a total assessment of $584,000. Hence, you can reasonably assume that 74% (432,160/584,000) of the total cost the property is represented by the depreciable building (see Chapter 34). You apply that 74% to the purchase price to estimate the dollar amount that you can depreciate. Assuming you begin with $765,000 as the purchase price, you would estimate the building's depreciable amount to be 74% of $765,000, or $566,100, and write that amount off over 39 years. Keep in mind that you can take only one-half month of depreciation in the month that the property is placed in service.

Your tenant improvement costs $3,000 and you put it in service in May, 2014. It will be in place for eight months that year and is similarly subject to the IRS's half-month convention, so you get 7.5 months of depreciation in the first year. A full year is 3,000 / 39 or about $79. Divide that by 12 and multiply by 7.5 to get the first-year amount of $48.

The new roof will go on at the beginning of 2018. The full-year amount of depreciation will be $1,026 (40,000 / 39), but for 2018 with the loss of one-half month, the amount will be $983.

4. You're going to pay the entire leasing commission of $4,284 in 2014, but you must spread the write-off over 60 months (the term of the lease), starting in May, 2014. $4,284 / 60 equals $71.40 per month, so you have eight months worth of deduction, $571, in 2014. For the next four years you write off 12 months each, or $857. That's a total of 56 months so there are still four months, or $256, to write off in 2019.

5. You paid two points to secure the first mortgage. Since you expect to finance 65% of the purchase price, the exact dollar amount of these points will depend on that purchase price. If the price is $765,000, then the mortgage will be 65% of that, or $497,250. Two points is 2% of that amount (see Chapter 27), or $9,945. You will pay that amount in its entirety when you close the loan, but you must amortize it over the 20-year term of the loan at $497 per year.

6. For simplicity, the previous case studies made only passing mention of closing costs you would pay to acquire a property. Of course real life won't be so gentle with you, so you estimate here that it will cost you $8,000 for legal fees, title insurance and the like. You will not be allowed to leave the closing under your own power unless the bill is paid in full, but the cost must be amortized over the useful life of the building, in this case 39 years.

    You will add the closing costs to the depreciable basis of the building before you calculate the actual depreciation deduction. From #3 above you know you can depreciate $566,100 for the building, to which you'll add $8,000 for the closing costs, totaling $574,100. Divide that by 39 years (the useful life of non-residential property according to the tax code du jour) and you have an annual depreciation deduction of $14,721 – except for the first year, when you lose half of the first month's depreciation.

    (Note: You also lose a half month of depreciation in the month that you sell or otherwise dispose of the property. In the pro formas that you see in this book, that half month is accounted for within the resale calculations.)

7. Finally, there is the matter of the interest rate on your mortgage. The problem states that the rate can adjust up to 1% per year, and that you do not expect it to increase above 11.5%. You need to make a crystal-ball judgment. You decide the rate will increase by 1% each year for three years, then by 0.5% so that it reaches 11.5% the fourth year; after that you believe it will remain level.

You should be ready now to build your standard income-property pro forma. Below, you see the calculation of taxable income.

	2014	2015	2016	2017	2018	2019	2020	2021	2022	2023
GROSS INCOME	130,191	140,017	143,308	148,343	156,612	159,294	161,365	172,544	177,986	184,707
- Vacancy & Credit Allowance	2,604	2,800	2,866	2,967	3,132	3,186	3,227	3,451	3,560	3,694
- Operating Expenses	47,743	49,730	52,129	53,956	55,946	57,842	59,794	62,091	64,300	66,631
NET OPERATING INCOME	79,845	87,487	88,312	91,420	97,534	98,266	98,344	107,002	110,127	114,382
Capitalization Rate	10.40%	11.39%	11.50%	11.90%	12.07%	12.16%	12.17%	13.24%	13.63%	14.16%
Debt Coverage Ratio	1.60	1.63	1.54	1.50	1.56	1.57	1.57	1.71	1.76	1.83
- Interest, First Mortgage	39,400	43,394	47,209	50,836	51,972	50,691	49,254	47,644	45,838	43,813
- Depreciation, Real Property	14,107	14,721	14,721	14,721	14,721	14,721	14,721	14,721	14,721	14,721
- Depreciation (39-year), Capital Improve.	0	0	0	0	983	1,026	1,026	1,026	1,026	1,026
- Depreciation, Tenant Improvements	48	77	77	77	77	77	77	77	77	77
- Amortization of Leasing Commissions	571	857	857	857	857	286	0	0	0	0
- Amortization of Points, 1st Mortgage	497	497	497	497	497	497	497	497	497	497
INCOME OR (LOSS)	25,221	27,942	24,952	24,433	28,428	30,969	32,769	43,038	47,968	54,249

This shows you some of the items that are new to this case study: depreciation of the combined real property and closing costs; depreciation of capital improvements for the property as a whole as well as for improvements made for a specific tenant; and amortization of leasing commissions and points.

When you examine this part of the pro forma you notice that your Debt Coverage Ratio is strong, starting at 1.60 and staying between 1.50 and 1.83 during the entire 10 years of your projections. With a DCR like that, you can make an effective case for financing.

Your also notice that your interest cost rises during the first four years. If you had a fixed-rate loan you would expect more money to go to principal each year and less to interest. But your loan is variable, and your forecast is for rising rates during the first four years. You did predict a level rate of interest after four years, so if that proves to be correct, then your loan will start to behave as if it were at a fixed rate and your annual interest costs will start to decline.

Because each of these assets is placed in service at a different time, you've accounted separately here for depreciation of the building, of the tenant improvements you make in the first year, and of the new roof (capital addition) you expect to put on in the fifth year. Likewise you've shown the amortization of leasing costs and loan points separately because they each have different start- and end-points.

Of course, every investor looks at the bottom line, in this case taxable income, and yours is positive. Next, you want to examine your projected cash flow.

	2014	2015	2016	2017	2018	2019	2020	2021	2022	2023
NET OPERATING INCOME	79,845	87,487	88,312	91,420	97,534	98,266	98,344	107,002	110,127	114,382
- Debt Service, First Mortgage	49,910	53,555	57,181	60,774	62,536	62,536	62,536	62,536	62,536	62,536
- Capital Additions	0	0	0	0	40,000	0	0	0	0	0
- Tenant Improvements	3,000	0	0	0	0	0	0	0	0	0
- Leasing Commissions	4,284	0	0	0	0	0	0	0	0	0
CASH FLOW BEFORE TAXES	22,650	33,932	31,132	30,646	(5,003)	35,730	35,807	44,465	47,590	51,846
Cash on Cash Return (CFBT/initial inv.)	7.93%	11.88%	10.90%	10.73%	-1.75%	12.51%	12.53%	15.56%	16.66%	18.15%
- Income Tax	7,062	7,824	6,987	6,841	7,960	8,671	9,175	12,051	13,431	15,190
CASH FLOW AFTER TAXES	15,588	26,109	24,145	23,805	(12,962)	27,058	26,632	32,415	34,159	36,656
Cumulative Cash Flow After Taxes	15,588	41,697	65,842	89,648	76,685	103,743	130,375	162,790	196,949	233,605

You can see immediately how some elements take on a different significance when looked at as cash flow items rather than as taxable income. Your capital additions (i.e., general improvements to the building), tenant improvements, and leasing commissions all impact your cash flow as soon as those costs are incurred; but they affect your taxable income, in small installments, as they are written off over time.

Notice that the loan points don't appear here. You might consider this omission a judgment call (and of course, since this is my book it is my judgment that prevails here). Inasmuch as you must typically pay the points on Day 1 at the closing – assuming the loan is being used to acquire the property – I think it is more appropriate to consider that outlay as part of your initial cash investment and not as part of your first-year cash flow. The same may be said of your closing costs, which also occur on Day 1. The difference is really nothing more than a matter of timing. Since you know that these funds are a cash outflow at the beginning of Year 1, that would appear to be the most appropriate place to put them when you perform a Discounted Cash Flow analysis.

The property seems to have a robust cash flow in every year except 2018. The reason for that, of course, is that you expect to spend $40,000 for a new roof in 2018, and the property is likely to generate only about $35,000 in cash that year. Hence, you will experience what investors refer to with ill humor as a "negative cash flow" – more cash going out than coming in.

In a real estate pro forma you might just leave a particular year's negative cash flow in place and move on to projection of the next year's performance. Regrettably, real life requires that you do more than that; you can't just leave your mortgage or taxes or lawn care unpaid and move on. You have to go outside the property's checkbook, reach into your own pocket and make up the difference.

If you think that a negative cash flow is unwelcome when you own a property as an individual, you can be sure that the unpleasantness will multiply if you have assembled an investment partnership to acquire the property and find yourself writing a letter asking the partners to kick in more cash to pay the bills. What to do?

When your projections suggest that one or more negative cash flows is possible – as well they might be if you anticipate a major cost such as a new roof – you would be wise to fund those negatives at the time you acquire the property. You can do that by establishing a "funded reserves" account. In addition to the capital needed to acquire the property, you also raise reserve funds that you set aside in an interest-bearing account, ready to be called upon to devour the negative cash flows. Your initial investment to acquire the property will be greater by the amount of those reserves; if you don't have to use all the money, you return it to the investors when you dispose of the property, or even earlier if you feel certain it won't be needed.

Let's see how this might work. You expect to have a negative cash flow in Year 5 (2018) of about $5,000, but you want to be cautious so you raise an extra $10,000 on Day 1. That money is now part of the initial cash investment needed to acquire this property – along with down payment, closing costs, and loan points. You put this cash into a money-market fund or CD earning 4% interest, and when it comes time to replace the roof, you tap this account to absorb what otherwise would have been a negative cash flow. So, in 2018 you use $5,003 from your reserve fund and end up with a zero cash flow for that year.

Thanks to the interest earned on your reserve fund, you still have $7,164 left over. You remain cautious, however, and choose to leave that balance in the fund, earning interest, for one more year, just in case some issue arises with new roof. At the end of 2019, you're confident that you can distribute the balance, now grown to $7,451.

Note that the only tax consequence of the reserve fund arises from the interest earned on the account. Otherwise, it was your (or your partnership's) own capital when you put it in and when you returned the excess. Your cash flow projections now look like this:

	2014	2015	2016	2017	2018	2019	2020	2021	2022	2023
NET OPERATING INCOME	79,845	87,487	88,312	91,420	97,534	98,266	98,344	107,002	110,127	114,382
- Debt Service, First Mortgage	49,910	53,555	57,181	60,774	62,536	62,536	62,536	62,536	62,536	62,536
- Funded Reserves	10,000	0	0	0	0	0	0	0	0	0
Interest Earned on Funded Reserves	400	416	433	450	468	287	0	0	0	0
- Capital Additions	0	0	0	0	40,000	0	0	0	0	0
- Tenant Improvements	3,000	0	0	0	0	0	0	0	0	0
- Leasing Commissions	4,284	0	0	0	0	0	0	0	0	0
CASH FLOW BEFORE TAXES	22,650	33,932	31,132	30,646	(5,003)	35,730	35,807	44,465	47,590	51,846
Cash on Cash Return (CFBT/Initial inve	7.66%	11.48%	10.53%	10.36%	-1.69%	12.08%	12.11%	15.04%	16.09%	17.53%
Reserves Utilized	0	0	0	0	5,003	7,451	0	0	0	0
Reserves Remaining	10,400	10,816	11,249	11,699	7,164	0	0	0	0	0
NET CASH FLOW AFTER RESERVES	22,650	33,932	31,132	30,646	0	43,180	35,807	44,465	47,590	51,846
- Income Tax Attributable to Property	7,174	7,940	7,108	6,967	8,091	8,752	9,175	12,051	13,431	15,190
CASH FLOW AFTER TAXES & RESRV.	15,476	25,992	24,024	23,679	(8,091)	34,428	26,632	32,415	34,159	36,656
Cumulative Cash Flow After Taxes	15,476	41,469	65,493	89,172	81,081	115,510	142,142	174,556	208,716	245,372

On the taxable income side, the only change is due to the six years that the reserve fund earned interest:

+ Interest, Funded Reserves	400	416	433	450	468	287
INCOME OR (LOSS)	25,621	28,358	25,384	24,883	28,896	31,256

Note that you used the reserve fund to zero out the Cash Flow Before Taxes. Personal income tax issues are external to the property; in other words, the property itself doesn't pay the income taxes. If this investment is indeed in the form of a limited partnership or LLC, the taxable income or losses are passed through to the individual investors and each is responsible for taxes on his or her share of the income or loss.

The final step in your pro forma analysis of this property is to look at the potential resale and the overall rates of return. Because this commercial property has involved a number of issues you haven't dealt with in the previous case studies – leasing commissions, tenant improvements, capital addition, loan points, and reserves to name just some – your resale analysis will have more of these issues to sort out.

To simplify matters, let's first break up the resale into two logical parts. You recall how, in your operating pro formas, you looked at the taxable income, then the cash flow. You can do the same for resale, focusing first on the taxable gain, then on the cash proceeds from the sale.

	2014	2015	2016	2017	2018	2019	2020	2021	2022	2023
PROJECTED SELLING PRICE	760,400	833,200	841,100	870,700	928,900	935,900	936,600	1,019,100	1,048,800	1,089,400
Selling Price Based on Capitalization Rate of 10.50%										
ORIGINAL BASIS, Purchase Price of R.E.	765,000	765,000	765,000	765,000	765,000	765,000	765,000	765,000	765,000	765,000
+ Closing Costs	8,000	8,000	8,000	8,000	8,000	8,000	8,000	8,000	8,000	8,000
+ Cumulative Capital Additions and T. I.	3,000	3,000	3,000	3,000	43,000	43,000	43,000	43,000	43,000	43,000
+ Costs of Sale	53,228	58,324	58,877	60,949	65,023	65,513	65,562	71,337	73,416	76,258
- Adjusted Cumulative Depreciation, R. E.	13,494	28,214	42,935	57,655	72,376	87,096	101,817	116,537	131,258	145,978
- Adjusted Cumulative Depr., Cap. Add.	0	0	0	0	942	1,966	2,991	4,017	5,043	6,068
- Adjusted Cumulative Depr., Tenant Impr.	46	122	199	276	353	429	506	583	660	737
ADJUSTED BASIS AT SALE	815,688	805,988	791,743	779,018	807,353	792,021	776,247	766,199	752,455	739,474
GAIN OR (LOSS) ON SALE, Real Estate	(55,288)	27,212	49,357	91,682	121,547	143,879	160,353	252,901	296,345	349,926
DEDUCTIONS AT SALE										
Suspended Losses Utilized upon Sale	0	0	0	0	0	0	0	0	0	0
Unamortized Loan Points	(9,448)	(8,951)	(8,453)	(7,956)	(7,459)	(6,962)	(6,464)	(5,967)	(5,470)	(4,973)
Unamortized Leasing Commissions	(3,713)	(2,856)	(1,999)	(1,142)	(286)	(0)	(0)	(0)	(0)	(0)
TOTAL DEDUCTIONS AT SALE	(13,161)	(11,807)	(10,452)	(9,098)	(7,744)	(6,962)	(6,464)	(5,967)	(5,470)	(4,973)
TOTAL FEDERAL TAX ON SALE	(4,353)	3,670	9,274	18,858	26,009	30,398	34,610	52,516	61,582	72,474

The amount of detail shown on the previous page may seem a bit daunting, but if you break it up into its logical parts, it should readily make sense. Remember that you are testing potential resale scenarios for each year. "What if I sell in 2014? What if I sell in 2015?" and so forth. Of course you can only really sell the property once (unless you're that guy with the Brooklyn Bridge) so ultimately you're going to narrow your focus to just one column.

The top half of the report displays three key components.

Projected Selling Price – Been here, done this lots of times before. It's Chapter 10 again, where you take the Net Operating Income and divide it by the cap rate to get an estimate of value. You already labored long and hard to get the expected NOI for each year, and the case study specified 10.5% as the cap rate, so this is simple division. If your assumptions and projections are valid, then the value of this property should grow to nearly $1.1 million by 2023.

Adjusted Basis – You covered this in Chapter 33. Start with the original basis (purchase price plus closing costs); add any capital additions or tenant improvements that you made while you owned the property; then subtract out all of the accumulated depreciation you have taken. Remember that you are allowed only one-half month of depreciation in the month you sell.

Gain or Loss – Find the difference between the two items above, as in Chapter 34, and that is your gain. Until and unless Congress changes the tax laws, if you've held the property for more than a year then this amount should be taxed at the capital gain rate, typically lower than the rate you would pay on ordinary income.

The gain is your profit from the sale of the property. As you can see, if you sell the property at the end of the second year or later then you'll make a profit – one that increases from about $27,000 for a sale at the end of 2015 to nearly $350,000 for a sale at the end of 2023.

The rest of the report is worth noting but perhaps not worth dwelling on too closely because the methods shown here are entirely a function of the tax code that is current at this writing. That code provides some opportunities for deductions at sale time. You may have had losses that were suspended in a prior year because they were too great or your income was too high. When you sell the property, you can take those previously-suspended losses. Also you may have been amortizing loan points and leasing commissions over the years, but still have a balance that remains unamortized. You can generally write that balance off when you sell. All of this is stirred in with your capital gains tax to come up with the total tax liability at the time of sale.

Again, be forewarned: The tax code changes frequently and provisions related to real estate may be different when you read this.

Thankfully, the laws of bookkeeping are far more permanent than those of the tax code and it is with those, shown in the second part of your resale projections, that you'll account for the cash you take home from the closing.

As before, you start with your property's projected selling price. You subtract the Costs of Sale (broker, attorney, etc.) and the debt you have outstanding on the property. In this case you have just a first mortgage. If you funded a reserve account, you're entitled to take the balance with you. It was your money when you put it in, so it is not subject to tax when you take it back.

Now you have your before-tax sale proceeds. If you believe you've made a credible estimate of the tax due on the sale, you can subtract that as well to get the after-tax sale proceeds.

	2014	2015	2016	2017	2018	2019	2020	2021	2022	2023
PROJECTED SELLING PRICE	760,400	833,200	841,100	870,700	928,900	935,900	936,600	1,019,100	1,048,800	1,089,400
- Costs of Sale	53,228	58,324	58,877	60,949	65,023	65,513	65,562	71,337	73,416	76,258
- First Mortgage Payoff, EOY	486,740	476,579	466,608	456,670	446,105	434,259	420,977	406,085	389,386	370,663
+ Balance of Reserve Fund	10,400	10,816	11,249	11,699	7,164	0	0	0	0	0
BEFORE-TAX SALE PROCEEDS	230,832	309,113	326,864	364,780	424,936	436,128	450,061	541,678	585,998	642,479
- Total Federal Tax on Sale	(4,353)	3,670	9,274	18,858	26,009	30,398	34,610	52,516	61,582	72,474
AFTER-TAX SALE PROCEEDS	235,185	305,443	317,590	345,922	398,927	405,730	415,451	489,163	524,416	570,005

As you look at these proceeds, both before and after taxes, you wonder how those amounts compare to your going-in cash. So, how much cash did you really invest to get into this deal?

Your presumed purchase price is $765,000, of which you financed 65%. That leaves 35% as your down payment, or $267,750. You also paid loan points and closing costs, and funded a reserve account. Add it all up:

Down payment	267,750
Loan points	9,945
Closing costs	8,000
Funded reserves	10,000
Total	295,695

From previous pro formas you've become accustomed to seeing poor results if you try to sell your income property within the first year, especially when paying full Costs of Sale. You find the same is true with this property, both in terms of your taxable gain and your cash proceeds. Once you get to the second year, however, you believe you will get more cash out at sale time than you put in.

So far, all the signals you've received about this property – debt coverage, cash flow, gain, sale proceeds – have been positive, provided you hold it at least two years. Now it's time to examine the rate-of-return metrics.

	2014	2015	2016	2017	2018	2019	2020	2021	2022	2023
Internal Rate of Return, before Tax	-14.28%	11.61%	12.87%	14.58%	14.90%	14.60%	14.22%	15.69%	15.80%	15.99%
Modified IRR, Before Tax	-14.28%	11.45%	12.43%	13.77%	13.81%	13.40%	12.92%	14.03%	13.95%	13.96%
Internal Rate of Return, after Tax	-15.23%	8.52%	9.54%	11.04%	11.37%	11.22%	10.94%	12.37%	12.53%	12.77%
Modified IRR, after Tax	-15.23%	8.48%	9.40%	10.70%	10.89%	10.57%	10.26%	11.42%	11.47%	11.59%
PV, NOI & Sale Price less Costs	712,232	778,519	789,116	813,809	854,257	861,985	865,765	907,275	922,841	941,162
PV, CFAT & Sale Proceeds after Taxes	226,843	285,446	288,485	301,003	306,219	305,858	302,752	330,872	338,221	348,236
EQUITY, excluding reserves	220,432	298,297	315,615	353,081	417,772	436,128	450,061	541,678	585,998	642,479
RETURN ON EQUITY (CFAT/Equity)	7.02%	8.71%	7.61%	6.71%	-3.13%	6.19%	5.92%	5.98%	5.83%	5.71%

As expected you find the IRR and MIRR below sea level if you sell in the first year, largely the effect of paying a full brokerage commission to dispose of the property before it has had a chance to generate much cash flow or to grow in value.

Recall from the chapter, "The Single Family, Redeveloped," that MIRR tends to be slightly more conservative than IRR. It uses a so-called "Safe Rate" which is the interest rate at which you put money aside, in a secure and liquid form, so that it can grow to meet the amounts needed to cover any negative cash flows. In this analysis you've assigned a Safe Rate of 4%, although once you put reserves in place you had no negative cash flows to deal with.

MIRR also uses a "Reinvestment Rate" (sometimes called the Risk Rate), which is the rate at which you assume you can reinvest all positive cash flows. This is an alternative to the assumption implicit in standard IRR that you can reinvest positive cash flows at the internal rate. Often, your yearly cash flows aren't large enough to command that kind of investment power, so a more conservative choice is needed. For this pro forma, you chose 7%.

The IRR and MIRR before taxes come in at double digits, showing slight dips in 2019 and 2020, then recovering. Why the dips? Your Net Operating Income grew by just a few hundred dollars in each of those years. Keep in mind the earlier discussion of time value of money. After you discount the slightly higher 2019 NOI for an additional year, it is worth less than the discounted 2018 NOI. The NOI for 2020 must be discounted for two additional years, so it is worth less still.

The after-tax IRR and MIRR take until the fourth year to break the double-digit threshold, but they mirror the generally upward trend over time. These rates of return aren't extravagant; no one should fault you for trying to improve them by negotiating a lower purchase price. This is a moment suited better to judgment than to mathematics. Do these rates of return and the time needed to achieve them meet your investment objectives? That's a subjective call, and it's yours to make.

You can slice and dice the numbers in a variety of additional ways, and perhaps that will help you decide how you feel about this opportunity. Back in "Single-Family, Redeveloped" you saw an approach favored by commercial appraisers, and shown next on the report. Take the Net Operating Income for each year you operate the property and the Gross Selling Price for the year of sale, and perform a Discounted Cash Flow analysis. (Note: Some analysts prefer to use a Net Selling Price, which is the gross price less Costs of Sale.)

Keeping the same 10.5% discount rate that you've used throughout this pro forma, you would find that the Present Value of the first year's income stream to be $760,402, certainly within a reasonable margin of error of the $765,000 that you paid for it. However, if you take into account the selling costs and use the Net Selling Price instead, then the Present Value of that first year's income stream drops to $712,232. If you hold for two years, it grows to $778,519. You've already seen that selling costs can skew the return on a property held for just one year. Once again, you have a judgment call to make. How concerned do you want to be about performance over just one year? There is no universal answer. Are there circumstances in your life that could compel you to dispose of the property sooner than you would like; or are you confident that you can invest for the long term?

Additional metrics abound. You can look at the Present Value of the after-tax cash flow and sale proceeds, and compare that to your initial cash investment. You might think of this measure as a companion to the after-tax IRR and MIRR. Note for example that your Present Value at the end of the second year, using a 10.5% discount rate, is $285,446. That amount is less than your initial cash investment of $295,695. Since the PV is less than your initial investment, that means you didn't really earn the discount rate of 10.5%. You earned the IRR (or MIRR, if you prefer) of about 8.5%.

The Return on Equity is another measure that can shed some light on how this income-property investment might play out (see Chapter 25). Equity, as used here, is not your original investment but rather the difference between the presumed value of the property, less Costs of Sale and the outstanding debt – in other words, the current but unrealized equity you have in the property. The "return" is the current year's cash flow after taxes.

In certain circumstances the measure may not be particularly meaningful. In 2018, your roof replacement blew the doors off your cash flow, causing a one-time negative ROE. However, you can sometimes detect a general downward trend with ROE, suggesting that your cash flow is not growing as quickly as your equity, perhaps due to amortization of your mortgages. If you see such a signal you may want to consider extracting some or all of that of that equity through a refinance or sale and leveraging the proceeds into additional or larger income property.

There are still more tools you can employ to help you reach a decision about this investment. A few pages ago, you were ruminating on the notion of offering less than $765,000 – the value suggested by applying the 10.5% cap rate. There are at least two techniques you could use to get a quick handle on the implications of alternative prices. One of these is a sensitivity analysis. Below you see a software-generated table that shows how the required cash investment, as well as Year 5 and Year 10 IRR after taxes, is sensitive to increases or decreases in the purchase price. In this example you've changed the price both up and down in increments of 2.5%.

Potential Purchase Price	Required Cash Investment	Year 5 IRR After-Tax	Year 10 IRR After-Tax
669,375	260,983	18.06%	16.44%
688,500	267,926	16.67%	15.66%
707,625	274,868	15.31%	14.90%
726,750	281,810	13.97%	14.17%
745,875	288,753	12.66%	13.47%
765,000	295,695	11.37%	12.77%
784,125	302,637	10.11%	12.08%
803,250	309,580	8.86%	11.41%
822,375	316,522	7.65%	10.75%
841,500	323,465	6.48%	10.10%
860,625	330,407	5.32%	9.46%

Another tool you can try is goal-seeking. What if you want to reverse-engineer your analysis and find the purchase price that would give you a before-tax IRR of 17% if you hold the property through 2018 (assuming, of course, that all your other assumptions remained unchanged)? Some analysis software can do this automatically, saving you a lot of trial and error. The answer is $739,603. Try it out.

You've dealt with a good deal of new material in this chapter. Let's review some of the key topics you covered:

1. You learned about the need to anticipate how major events – including some external to the property itself – might impact the

course of your investment. In this case, you recognized that local school construction was bound to impact your future property taxes. You also acknowledged that buildings wear out over time, and therefore budgeted the cost of a new roof.

2. You learned some new ways of looking at revenue that are characteristic of commercial property. In particular, you saw the importance of projecting the rent and certain costs on a unit-by-unit basis. Commercial tenants typically pay on a per-square-foot basis and have leases that are longer than those in residential property, often with built in rent escalations. You saw the importance of forecasting the likelihood of lease renewals and the need to plan for rollover vacancy when renewal of a particular lease was questionable. Another source of revenue that you encountered for the first time was pass-through income, a tenant's obligation to reimburse you for part or all of certain operating expenses.

3. You calculated depreciation allowance for the primary improvement – the building – and learned to take the half-month convention into account. You also found that it may be necessary to depreciate improvements made after acquisition, such as a new roof or an upgrade to a particular tenant's space.

4. In regard to cash outflow, you dealt with tenant improvements (i.e., capital improvements made for the benefit of specific tenants), and leasing commissions; and you found that both of these are typically capital items and not operating expenses. You worked with loan points and closing costs, also capital items.

5. You saw how you might plan ahead for major costs in the future by funding a reserve account at the time of acquisition; and you considered how important this might be in particular when structuring a partnership with other investors.

6. You reviewed some new metrics, such as MIRR, the Present Value of the income stream, and Return on Equity.

7. You looked at sensitivity analysis as a means visualizing the relationship between IRR and purchase price, and considered goal-seeking as a way to identify the purchase price that would yield a required rate of turn.

INDEX

A

Adjusted Basis, ii, 136, 137, 138, 143, 144, 145, 165, 238
Allowance
  Depreciation, 141
amortization, 49, 121, 122, 124, 125, 126, 129, 231, 244
Amortization of Points, 44, 46, 47, 48, 50
amortized, 49, 124, 190, 221, 229
annual depreciation deduction, 229
Annual Property Operating Data, 31, 160, 190, 224
apartment, 2, 17, 18, 19, 31, 87, 140, 155, 156, 157, 161, 173, 187, 188, 189, 200, 205, 210, 227
APOD, 31, 32, 33, 34, 35, 160, 161, 189, 190, 191, 219, 225
Appraised Value, 134, 135
appreciation rate, 166, 167, 169, 177
Assessed Value, ii, 134, 135
Assessment Ratio, 134, 135

B

back-door approach, 173
balloon payment, 120
BER, 101, 104
Break-Even Ratio, ii, 101, 102, 103, 104, 109
brokerage commission, 65, 76, 243

C

Capital Additions, 44, 46, 47, 48, 50, 51, 53, 54, 136, 137, 138, 144, 145
capital improvements, 31, 45, 49, 136, 231, 246
Capital Improvements, 136
Capitalization Rate, i, 37, 38, 39, 40, 41, 42, 66, 67, 68, 78, 108, 178, 192, 227
Cash Flow, i, 1, 2, 9, 17, 31, 35, 51, 52, 53, 54, 55, 56, 57, 58, 59, 60, 61, 62, 63, 70, 71, 72, 73, 74, 75, 77, 79, 80, 81, 84, 85, 86, 106, 107, 108, 162, 163, 181, 182, 189, 193, 195, 233, 236, 244
  Discounted, 70, 79
Cash-on-Cash Return, i, 59, 60, 61, 62, 63
CD, 234
Closing Costs, 44, 46, 47, 48, 50
commercial lease analysis, 227
Commercial tenant, 246
commission
  brokerage, 65
compound interest, 1, 4, 9, 11, 28
Cost Approach, 15
Costs of Sale, 64, 65, 66, 67, 68, 73, 78, 136, 137, 138, 143, 144, 145, 181, 184, 185, 186, 239, 241, 244
Credit Loss
  Vacancy and, 51
Credit Loss Allowance, i, 22, 29, 32, 34, 38

D

DCR, 97, 98, 99, 100, 162, 174, 195, 231
Debt Coverage Ratio, ii, 97, 98, 99, 100, 101, 109, 130, 131, 132, 162, 172, 174, 180, 188, 195, 201, 231
Debt Service, 51, 53, 54, 55, 56, 57, 60, 61, 62, 77, 97, 98, 100, 101, 102, 103, 104
Default Ratio, 101
depreciable amount, 228
depreciable building, 228
depreciation, 15, 31, 36, 46, 48, 49, 52, 136, 137, 139, 140, 141, 142, 143, 144, 184, 196, 205, 227, 228, 229, 231, 238, 246
Depreciation, ii, 32, 35, 44, 46, 47, 48, 49, 50, 136, 137, 138, 139, 140, 141, 142, 144, 145, 162
Discounted Cash Flow, 244

E

Effective Gross Income, i, 27
Equity Dividend Rate, 59
Excel, 10, 11, 12, 71, 84, 85, 86, 116, 117, 118, 119, 121, 122, 123, 124, 127
Expenses per Square Foot, ii, 89, 90
Expenses per Unit, i, 87, 88
Extermination, 207, 222

F

financing
  commercial, 162
front-door approach, 173, 185
funded reserves account, 233
Future Value, 4, 5, 6, 9, 10, 11, 12, 28, 29

G

Gain on Sale, ii, 143, 144, 145, 165, 189, 196
GOI, 33, 34, 56, 94, 96, 103, 225
GRM, 13, 14, 15, 16
Gross Building Area, 89, 90, 91, 149, 150, 151
Gross Operating Income, i, 27, 28, 29, 30, 39, 44, 45, 47, 48, 49, 51, 53, 54, 55, 56, 57, 60, 61, 62, 65, 67, 68, 92, 94, 95, 99, 101, 102, 103, 104, 132, 174, 201, 224, 225
Gross Rent Multiplier, i, 13, 14, 15, 16
Gross Schedule Income, 20, 30, 32
Gross Scheduled Income, i, 13, 14, 15, 16, 17, 18, 19, 21, 22, 24, 25, 27, 28, 29, 30, 32, 33, 34, 38, 39, 44, 51, 53, 54, 55, 56, 57, 58, 87, 88, 89, 90, 91, 93, 94, 95, 99, 102, 103, 131, 132, 174, 190, 191
Gross Scheduled Rent, 201
Gross Selling Price, 243

H

half-month convention, 139, 140, 141, 228, 246
House
  Single-Family, 155

I

imputed interest, 177
Income Approach, 15
inspections, 176
insurance, 159, 172, 174, 188, 191, 192, 211, 225, 229
Interest
  Mortgage, 46

Interest Earned, 44, 45, 46, 47, 48,
    50, 51, 53, 54
interest rate, 243
Internal Rate of Return, i, 84, 85, 86,
    165, 169, 181, 186, 189, 196
IRR, 84, 85, 86, 165, 166, 169, 181,
    182, 184, 186, 196, 197, 199, 243,
    244, 245, 246

L

leasing commission, 207, 228
limited partnership, 236
LLC, 236
Loan Proceeds, 51, 53, 54
Loan-to-Value Ratio, ii, 101, 109,
    110, 111, 112, 131, 133, 172, 175,
    195
LTV, 109

M

market capitalization rate, 37, 107
Market Data Approach, 15
Market Value, 13, 14, 15, 16
Maximum Loan Amount, ii, 130,
    131, 132, 174, 175
MIRR, 181, 182, 184, 186, 199, 243,
    244, 246
mixed-use project, 18
Modified Internal Rate of Return,
    181
Mortgage, ii, 32, 44, 46, 47, 48, 49,
    52, 61, 62, 64, 65, 66, 67, 68, 73,
    74, 78, 93, 106, 107, 108, 113,
    114, 115, 116, 117, 118, 120, 122,
    130, 131, 132, 174
Mortgage Constant, ii, 115
Mortgage Interest, 32, 44, 46, 47, 48,
    49, 93

N

Net Income Multiplier, i, 42, 43
Net Operating Income, i, 30, 31, 32,
    35, 37, 38, 39, 40, 41, 42, 43, 44,
    45, 46, 47, 48, 49, 51, 52, 53, 54,
    55, 56, 57, 59, 60, 61, 62, 65, 66,
    67, 68, 76, 77, 78, 94, 97, 98, 99,
    100, 107, 108, 130, 131, 132, 157,
    162, 174, 178, 183, 189, 191, 192,
    201, 209, 225, 227, 238, 243
Net Present Value, 75, 79, 84
Net Rentable Area, 89, 90, 91
NIM, 42, 43
NOI, 30, 31, 33, 34, 35, 37, 38, 39,
    42, 43, 56, 60, 67, 68, 78, 97, 99,
    100, 157, 160, 161, 174, 177, 178,
    179, 182, 183, 184, 186, 189, 192,
    195, 196, 198, 201, 225, 227, 238,
    243
non-residential, 20, 45, 46, 49, 139,
    141, 227, 229
NPV, 75, 76, 77, 79, 80, 81, 82

O

office buildings, 156, 172, 206
Operating Expense Ratio, ii, 92, 93,
    94, 95
Operating Expenses, 30, 39, 44, 47,
    48, 49, 51, 53, 54, 55, 56, 57, 61,
    62, 67, 68, 87, 88, 89, 90, 99, 100,
    101, 102, 103, 104, 132, 174, 208
Original basis, 136, 137, 138, 144,
    145
Outstanding Principal Balance, 126,
    127, 128
owner-occupied, 15, 156

P

Periodic Payment, 121, 122, 123

permits, 172
Pest Control, 207, 222
PMT, 116, 117, 118, 119, 123, 127
Points, ii, 45, 113, 114
    Amortization of, 44, 50
    Dollar Amount of, 114
Potential Gross Income, i, 17
Present Value, i, 9, 10, 11, 12, 70, 72,
    73, 74, 75, 76, 77, 79, 80, 81, 82,
    84, 116, 117, 118, 119, 120, 125,
    127, 165, 182, 198, 244, 246
    Net, 75
Profitability Index, i, 80, 81, 82
pro-forma analysis, 177
property
    Commercial, 90
PV, 9, 10, 11, 12, 70, 71, 73, 74, 76,
    79, 81, 115, 116, 117, 120, 121,
    122, 123, 182, 244

R

Reinvestment Rate, 243
Repairs and Maintenance, 31, 32, 93,
    94, 95, 98, 99, 188, 208
Return on Equity, ii, 106, 107, 108,
    165, 244, 246
Risk Rate, 243
Rule of 72s, i, 7

S

Sale Proceeds, i, 64, 65, 66, 67, 68,
    69, 73, 74, 77, 78, 164, 165, 168,
    189, 196

Selling Price, 14, 15, 64, 65, 66, 67,
    68, 73, 78, 109, 110, 111, 112,
    133, 143, 144, 145, 168, 175, 238,
    243, 244
shopping centers, 156
Simple Interest, i, 1
single-family homes, 15
Single-Family House, ii, 155
soft costs, 172, 176, 177, 178
software, 2, 159, 167, 179, 210, 221,
    245

T

tax liability, 52, 58, 64, 65, 68, 184,
    239
Taxable Income, i, 44, 46, 47, 48, 50
taxes, 52, 54, 58, 59, 159, 165, 168,
    169, 172, 174, 180, 181, 182, 188,
    191, 192, 206, 207, 208, 211, 219,
    225, 233, 236, 241, 243, 244, 245,
    246
top-down approach, 55

V

Vacancy and Credit Loss, i, 22, 25,
    27, 28, 29, 30, 32, 34, 38, 39, 44,
    51, 53, 54, 55, 56, 57, 94, 95, 99,
    102, 103, 132, 174, 209

Z

zoning, 172, 176